"It's time to change your story. That is the message of Kirstin Leigh. In a time when so many people are finding themselves in an OK life, Kirstin Leigh tells us and shows us by experience that there is definitely more. Her story is compelling and gives us hope, that we can change the channel at any point in our journey and find a life full of meaning and strength. I highly recommend this encouraging book."
—**Tim Storey**, Author, Speaker, Life Advisor

"*Change Your Story* will give you the impetus and inspiration you need to get you 'unstuck' and make those long desired changes in your life! Full of Biblical truths and powerful insights, Kirstin Leigh will help you shake off your past, alter your thinking, and dare to believe that you DO have a wonderful future and destiny. A natural encourager, Kirstin proves that it doesn't matter where you've been—you CAN change your story! This book can change your life!"
—**Nancy Stafford**, Actress, Speaker, and Author of *The Wonder of His Love: A Journey into the Heart of God* and *Beauty by the Book: Seeing Yourself as God Sees You.*

"Everyone has a story but only the brave really share their stories. Kirstin Leigh is brave. I know her. She is radiant, life-giving, a blessing bearer to all. She is a woman who has learned to live again and her life message will inspire, motivate, and equip you to change your story. Her practical insights will engage you and give you the courage to dig deeply into your own story. You will start to see it from a new perspective. This book will read you as you read it providing onramps to a road of unimaginable freedom where dreams become reality. I am honored to endorse such a life giving book."
—**W. Rex Holt**, Pastor of Mercy Chapel, Agoura Hills, CA

"*Change Your Story* is not just another information-filled, pull yourself up by the boot straps, self-help book. It's a real live drama with lots of pain and heart-ache, but then practical steps of how to get healing, freedom, and victory. Kirstin's story may look like a beautiful, colorful tapestry on the front side, but when you turn it over, as in most of our lives, you see all the knots and broken threads that have been weaved together by the Maker's kind, loving hands. She will inspire and challenge you to "let God work all things together for good and for His purpose."
—**Judy Radachy**, Founder & Co-Director of Oasis of Hollywood.

You don't have to live with whatever life throws you—
or whatever you've gotten yourself into

CHANGE YOUR STORY

Your Life is a Masterpiece Waiting to be Discovered

KIRSTIN LEIGH

In Honor of Jesus Christ, my Lord and Savior

To The One who saw my truth, as well as my pain. The only One I could not hide from. Thank you for never letting me go. For never letting me be satisfied. In seeking You, I found me. The real me that was dying to live. Thank You for saving me, for using me, for trusting me. I pray my words bring You glory, and help set Your people free.

This book is also dedicated to my mom.

I know this book has not been an easy read—you have read and re-read chapters of my life that you never knew existed. Yet you never complained. You just kept encouraging, removing commas, and listening to my heart. Thank you for your heart. It spoke to me when you didn't, when you couldn't. Your love made me want to change. Thank you for letting me find my way; for loving, forgiving, and growing with me. You are one of the greatest gifts God ever gave me, and I love you with every part of my being. May we forever seek to follow our story.

CONTENTS

Acknowledgments

Kimber, Indigo, my Schnook, and sister—God put us together on purpose. Thank you for the light, love, and wisdom which is you.

Leslie Gant, Melissa Nunnally, Fiona Gibson, Amy Graeser Andréa Mahee, and Mary Huckstep—thank you for encouraging, advising, editing, and making me smile along the way.

Holly—this book is for you. I love you and I believe in you.

Aaron and Katie Sturm of Holistech Systems, and Elizabeth Owens—thank you for creating my website. Gregory Patrick and Tim Thompson—thank you for blessing me with photos and footage. I'd also like to acknowledge Chris Cotton who came along at just the right time. Each of you are an answer to prayer and a reminder that God works in mysterious ways.

Michael Hevesy, my photographer. Thank you, once again, for being a part of a dream bigger than me. You were there from the beginning, and I cherish our friendship.

Dad—I love you and am always here for you.

Tim Storey, Beth Moore, Joyce Meyer, Dr. Caroline Leaf, Cindy Trimm, and Carter Conlon. Thank you for following God's call on your life. Your wisdom, words, and messages helped me "change my story."

For my prayer warriors at Warner Brothers 9t5, my friends near and far, and for every stranger who walked into my life at the perfect time—thank you.

For the amazing authors, speakers, and pastors who endorsed this book. I'm blessed, honored, and humbled.

INTRODUCTION

Do you feel like there is more to life than you are living? Is your strength wearing out? Are you tired of fighting the same battles, barely getting by? Do you struggle with your past? Wrestle with an addiction? Maybe you can't identify with any of these things. Maybe your life is great and you feel guilty for even picking up this book. But if truth be told, somewhere along life's way, you lost a little bit of you.

You don't have to live with whatever life throws you (or whatever you've gotten yourself into). You can change your story! God has a purpose and plan for your life that is greater than you can possibly imagine. But you have to believe it. And you have to fight for it.

I spent half my life keeping secrets. I'm sharing them so you don't have to make the same mistakes I did—or at least not live with them for as long as I did. You don't have to let "where you are" become who you are. You don't have to sink in your setback. You don't have to settle, living a "less than" life, being a "less than" you.

I am a Christian. One who lived without letting God be the God of my life for many years. Even when I desperately wanted to, even when I thought I was—I wasn't. On the outside, things looked fine. No one knew about my depression, my loneliness, my anxiety, the eating disorder that plagued my teenage years, or the alcohol that had become my secret companion. I didn't talk about my daddy issues, my fears, or how broken my "beautiful" heart was. Most people saw what they—and I—wanted them to see. A carefree, bubbly, "full of positivity" girl. Only God and my journals knew the truth.

This book is hard for me to write. I never shared my issues with anyone when I was hurting, so why now? I have conquered all this! And that is why I have to. God saved me so He could work through me.

I'm not some motivational cheerleader. Every insight, revelation, and piece of wisdom I'm sharing, I fought for. When I say that you are not your addiction, your problem, your pain, or your past—I know what I'm talking about. No matter where you are right now, or how many times you've fallen, it is not too late for you to change your story. As a matter of fact, it is time for your breakthrough.

Change Your Story opens yours eyes, enabling you to break free from habits, strongholds, lifestyles, and mindsets that are holding you back. By understanding spiritual warfare and the power in your words and thoughts, you will learn to let go of lies, re-train your brain, and uncover the hope that is buried beneath your pain. You can start over, trust yourself again, and use every mistake you've made to help others.

By grace, I had the opportunity to turn my life around—but I put myself in situations that could have ended with my not having that chance. It's called consequences. Every decision we make has them, and we never know when that last wrong decision will be the last one we ever make.

We all have our own journey. Our own road to recovery. To our destiny. I hope that by sharing pieces of mine, you will find yours. That something I say refreshes, revives, and reignites the hero inside you. That you discover or re-discover who you truly are and become everything God created you to be.

> *But those who hope in the Lord will renew their strength. They will soar on wings like eagles; they will run and not grow weary, they will walk and not be faint (Isaiah 40:31 NIV).*

1

A Little About Me

Don't let where you are determine who you are.

I'm from a very small town in Kentucky. Nothing about my environment said, "You can do whatever you set your mind to, just be yourself!" It was quite the opposite. I never fit in and was reminded of it daily. I acted like the constant bullying, threats, and insults didn't faze me. But they did. They made me question everything I did, and created an ongoing fear based dialogue in my head. Living in an anxiety state—with a smile on my face—was normal.

Despite all of this, I never stopped believing in myself. I was going to be a singer and an actress. However, the county I'm from is known for sports and beauty pageants (as well as drugs and teenage pregnancies), not the performing arts. Occasionally, there would be a talent competition, and I'd prepare my "you have to let me sing" speech like I was a lawyer fighting for my client's life.

I was at home on stage. The lights shining in my eyes, the anticipation—I loved all of it. My favorite part was watching the shift in people. Their eyes got lighter. Brighter. It was as if something in my voice woke up the hope in them.

When I sang, it felt like I could change the world. And I really wanted to change it. I practiced all the time, and dreamed of one of my favorite artists finding me and whisking me away from my small town. That never happened. But I did start babysitting when I was twelve, saved almost every penny I made, and moved to NYC when I was seventeen.

I was ready to conquer the world. However, there were times when the world almost conquered me. I had big dreams, but no strategy. A lot of talent, but no one to guide me. I had a good heart—with a lot of broken pieces. I had always gone to church, but I didn't understand that whether it's surviving the 4th grade or believing in your dreams when your world is falling apart, that God is always the answer.

Now if you had told me this, I would have nodded my head and said, "I know." But the truth is, I didn't know. I thought God was like my dad. That He was there for me when I was good, but when I didn't please him… not so much. I viewed myself, my worth, my everything, on how my dad, not God, saw me. And I made decisions accordingly.

The sting of life controlled my thoughts. And my thoughts controlled my life. If I had known about spiritual warfare, the power in prayer, that healing is real, and that our words carry energy… if I had admitted I was hurting, trusted my instincts, gotten to truly know God and who I am in Him—you would be reading a different story.

I don't believe "everything is meant to be." I believe God wants to direct our steps, but our free will makes for a lot of detours. God has a plan, but we have to get on board with Him in order for it to manifest. That being said, God can work everything out for our good. When we use our free will in the right way—cooperating, and co-creating with Him, He will restore the years we've sown in tears. The days ahead can be greater than our past. But we have to believe it. And we have to fight for it.

Some of you were born fighting. Love seems like a distant lie. A fairytale you hear in passing. "Why me?" echoes in your heart and plays its off-key tune in every decision you make. Defense has become your clothing, your armor.

Come to me, all you who are weary and burdened, and I will give you rest. Take my yoke upon you and learn from me, for I am gentle and humble in heart, and you will find rest for your souls (Matthew 11:28–29 NIV).

Growing up, I didn't realize that my problems stemmed from bigger issues. For instance, my eating disorder was a way for me to prove I was strong, and that I could do anything I set my mind to. (Along with good looks, this was very important to my dad.) It gave me control—until it controlled me. It started in tenth grade, when I got Bell's palsy.

Bell's palsy is a condition that causes the facial muscles to weaken or become paralyzed. It affects .02% of the population and is even less likely to occur in children and teens. I was on a double date, putting lipstick on when I noticed that my lipstick looked funny. The next morning I mentioned to mom that something was wrong with my mouth and I needed dad (who was a dentist) to look at my retainer. Then I ran out the door because I was already late for school.

The next morning I was adamant. Now parents are used to their kids yapping about their latest tragedy and mine were no different. Yet I will never forget the fear on my dad's face when he said, "I think you have Bell's palsy."

I didn't know what that was, but it did not sound good. I reminded myself that Dad could fix anything. He did miracles with people's teeth. One time he even sewed up my finger and put in seven stitches while I was sitting in his dental chair. He could fly an airplane. . . He understood geometry… "What's Bell's palsy?"

A trip to the emergency room confirmed that I had Bell's palsy. I was given steroids, but there was no guarantee they would actually help. By that afternoon, I couldn't raise my eyebrow, close my eye, my mouth—the whole left side of my face was frozen. All I could think of was "How am I going to be an actress? I need my mouth to move right to sing. How did I get this? Why is this happening?" I prayed and pleaded for God to take it away. I knew one thing—I had to be more than just "pretty." I was *more*, but my looks were the first thing people noticed. I liked the compliments, but I hated that sometimes it was all they saw. I especially hated it when people made fun of others. I always defended them, even if I didn't know who they were talking about. Now I was the one being made fun of.

My friends thought I was brave for going to school. School had been hell for years. There was no such thing as cyberbullying, but I was threatened by a select group of girls on a daily basis. Anyway, I didn't see attending school as "brave." I knew that even if my parents let me stay home, that they'd eventually make me go back and it would just make it harder. As it was, "the girls" brought their cameras to school, and laughing loudly, took pictures of me. This was the least of my concerns.

Thank God, after two long months, I was healed completely.

I was so happy to be healed that until it was pointed out to me, I didn't notice that I had gained some weight due to the steroids I had been on. Weight was one of the few things I never worried about. "How much do you weigh?" someone close to me asked.

"108 pounds," I replied.

"Not anymore you don't," commented the person. "Get on the scales."

Holy cow. I weighed 113 pounds. "Oh, well," I said reaching for a cookie, almost in defiance.

I went down to my natural 108 pounds easily. I stayed there for a while. But then my boyfriend, who I was very much in love with, broke up with me. (I soon found out he had been cheating on me with a friend.) The mean girls at school had gotten meaner, and my relationship with my dad was rockier. I don't know if it was a conscious decision or not, but I started eating less.

Everyone loved and admired my dad, and I was no exception. But he was a "my way or the highway" type person. My mom and my sister, Kimber, were natural pleasers. I wanted to please him too! But I didn't always agree with him. I asked "why" a lot and had my own opinions. He considered this "back talk" and most of our conversations ended in a fight. (Don't get me wrong, I was not the stellar child. There were definitely times when I was in the wrong. But never enough to warrant the many wrongs I will never write about.) When all four of us were together, something I'd say would inevitably result in him pitching a fit, my mom getting upset, my sister wanting to take my side, yet not wanting to be treated like me… it was easier for everyone if I just kept to myself.

The only time I didn't feel completely alone was when I was reading or writing. I'd bury myself in a book, becoming the character, living a life that mattered. I didn't know it then, but writing was a saving grace. It brought me closer to God than church did at that point.

Now the good thing about staying home and not going on family outings and vacations is that it gave me freedom to be me. I'd turn the house into a stage the minute everyone left. I'd stand at the top of the stairs reciting scenes from my countless acting books, dance through the living room, and work on songs. Anything to prepare myself for the future. I couldn't wait for the day when I would be around other people with big dreams. People who understood.

Soon, I'd be so happy from all the endorphins that come from doing what you love, that I'd think maybe things could be different. *Surely when Dad hears me sing this new song... Surely when...* As soon as my parents got home, I'd serenade them.

Though Dad encouraged my singing as a hobby, his response was always, "I hope you grow out of this."

Why would he want me to grow out of being me? I was so sick of not being taken seriously!

"You look great," Dad said when I had gotten down to 103 pounds. "I'm proud of you."

In my mind, this meant that my dad was finally taking me seriously. Pretty soon I weighed 98 pounds. And thus began the cycle that would haunt me for years. I gained and lost 20 plus pounds over and over again. I'd promise myself "I'd be good," which meant barely eating anything. If I was good, I'd reward myself by eating something I really liked. Five minutes later, a horrible shame would come over me, and I'd shove food in my mouth uncontrollably. Afterwards, I'd swear "no more," and for a while, I'd listen to myself. I never understood the "for a while," part. I prayed about it all the time, but my weapons were self-control and will power. What was making me do this? It wasn't me! Yet it was.

If this were a memoir, I'd share the details of the next few years. But it's not—*Change Your Story* is for you. My dreams, detours, tragedies, and triumphs just serve as the backdrop, so let's skip ahead to the ones that aid in Changing Your Story.

2

Addiction—the Biggest Distraction

"I have the right to do anything," you say— but not everything is beneficial. "I have the right to do anything"— but I will not be mastered by anything (1 Corinthians 6:12 NIV).

As I mentioned, I moved to NYC soon after high school. Everyone walked and talked as fast as I did. They were brave and exciting and… I felt more at home in New York City within the first five minutes than I ever had in Kentucky. By the end of the first month, I had found three jobs (going home was not an option), and made great friends. I was alive like never before! But secretly, I was still fighting the same battles.

I'll never forget the day it changed. All my friends were out having fun. I was in the apartment hiding. Crying. Stuffing myself with food I didn't like or want. *"You're killing yourself,"* said a voice from deep inside. This voice wasn't the demanding, pretending-to-be-nice one that said, *"You deserve this,"* then later filled me with shame. This voice was quiet. Serious. Almost sad. *"I gave you a beautiful body."* I hated that I had messed up my perfectly good body. But until that moment, I hadn't thought of it as a sin—just this huge blob of ugliness that wouldn't leave me alone.

I don't remember exactly what I said, but I remember standing in the kitchen and crying out like never before. "God, I can't live like this anymore. I give up. I can't do it! Please take this from me! I'm not strong enough. Please help me. I need you. I'm so sorry. Please forgive me. Save me from this, once and for all!" Something in the room changed. Almost like wind blowing in. Then right back out.

I had no idea what had happened, but something was very different. *It was over.* That self-sabotaging, "Do what I say," voice was gone. Like out-the-door gone.

I had been delivered. Mind you, I had no idea what "delivered" meant at the time. But I knew God had heard my cry. He had set me free.

Learning to live in that freedom was a journey. The compulsion to stuff myself was gone, but because I didn't deal with my backstory (which we will talk about later), circumstances, negative emotions, and unacknowledged feelings, still played a part in my decisions. In other words, the addiction was gone, but I didn't always live in the freedom God gave me.

This book isn't about addictions. It's about becoming the best version of yourself. But addictions, no matter what they are, will always be in the way of this happening.

Some addictions are deadly. All addictions are a distraction from our destiny. We can't hear God's voice, much less focus on our purpose (or discover what it is), when we are consumed with thoughts like, "Does anyone know? Can anyone tell? Tomorrow I'll be better. Just one more! I swear I won't…"

Throughout this book, I use food and alcohol as examples because that is I what I struggled with. But you can be addicted to people, thoughts, having fun, spending money, shopping, social media, soap operas, cleaning, volunteering—you can even be addicted to your recovery group. In other words, addictions don't limit themselves to the ones we constantly hear about in the media: drugs, alcohol, pornography, and sex. In fact, one of the most common roadblocks to changing your story is busyness. Busyness is addiction all dressed up. It's easy to ignore, because unlike other addictions, we don't see the problem—we see the accomplishments. But like everything else we hide behind, the "pay off" wears off. We always want more. And more is never enough.

The list of things you can be addicted to is endless. And regardless of how beautiful, loving, smart, or successful you are—no matter how well you hide and handle them, addictions color everything in your life.

"God, forgive us for what we do, and forgive us for what we don't do." I heard someone say that one night, and it really hit home. I used to look at people who drank and acted stupid and think, "Thank God that is not me." Yet how many times did I stay home and miss events that I wanted and needed to attend, because I was afraid it would be me looking stupid.

Your addiction is your addiction. It doesn't matter how it compares to others, nor does it have to fit any specific criteria. (None of mine did.) You don't have to be anorexic or bulimic to have an eating disorder. You don't have to be an alcoholic to be addicted to alcohol. Don't let anyone talk you in, or out, of thinking that you don't have a problem.

Talk to a pastor, a friend, someone who has *been* where you are. If you aren't familiar with the twelve steps, look them up. They can be applied to most every aspect of life. Check out an anonymous organization. There is one for every substance, emotion, compulsion, and addiction you could possibly have. Call one. Visit one. You don't have to go back, just try it.

All of the above things helped me—but Jesus healed me. He is the Greatest Counselor of all times. And I am here to tell you that *with Him* you can do all things.

> Your bad decisions can make your wiser.
> Your rocky past can clear the path
> for a purpose filled life.

Whether you are just beginning to notice a problem or you've fallen down and given up too many times to count, you can win this. For just "getting by," is not what God intended when He gave His one and only Son for us.

Addiction steals the life out of you. And the longer you live with it, the more of you it steals. John 10:10 tells us that the thief (aka, the devil, our enemy) comes only to kill, steal, and destroy, but that Jesus comes to give us an abundant life. An abundant life is not an "I'm okay, got nothing to complain about" life. It is an "overflowing with goodness, free to soar on wings like eagles" life.

The good news about addictions is that they aren't final. They are an opportunity to begin again.

Are you ready for an abundant life?

Dear God, I'm done with this addiction. No longer will I allow the enemy to have his way with me. I surrender my addiction, problems, heartache... every bit of me to You. I know I can't do this alone, but with Your strength I can say "no more" to every substance, voice, person, circumstance, and lifestyle that is not of You. I ask, and thank You in advance, for renewing my mind. For this "no" is merely a YES to You and all the amazing things You have in store for me.

You knew me before time began, and have plans to prosper, not to harm me, and to give me a hope and a future. Father, forgive me for everything I have done, and everything that I have left undone. I am ready to do things Your way. I choose You, and thank You so much for choosing me, for not giving up on me, for forgiving me, for aligning my will with Yours. I ask and thank You for Your supernatural protection, guidance and love. By the blood of Jesus, I am free.

3

The Hurricane

*There are many types of storms: there are natural
storms, spiritual storms, storms we bring on ourselves…
and then there are the storms that other people cause.*

I loved New York, but I was tired of living on friends'
couches. It was also the coldest, longest winter the city
had experienced in years, so when I read an article about
how many movies were being made in Miami and how it was
the new hot spot for actors, I thought, *This is perfect! I'll move
to Florida!*

If I were to have researched this a little, I would have
found out this was not exactly the case, but since I didn't have
long-term vision then, and wanted to believe it was true, I
moved. I liked having my own apartment, but I missed the
energy and hustle of New York.

I landed small parts in big movies and some starring roles in independent ones that never came to fruition. I was singing with a Top 40 band when Kimber decided to take a break from college and come live with me. Now, this was awesome!

She had just moved in, when a record-breaking hurricane threatened to destroy Miami. Our parents had retired and moved to central Florida, so we jumped in the car and sped off to safety.

Little did we know the "hurricane" we were in for.

"Many years ago, I had an affair. It's very possible you girls have a half-sister," said our dad. Kimber sat there, shocked. He had been the perfect dad to her. Everything she knew to be true about our family was a lie. For me, it was horrible, but in a completely different way. Like I touched on earlier, I saw a different side of him and my parents' marriage than anyone else did. I often wondered if that's why he got so mad at me. Because somehow, I knew he wasn't the perfect person everyone else thought he was.

My heart broke for my Mom. She's the most loving person you could ever meet. She makes everyone feel special. She's funny, talented, absolutely beautiful… and she catered to his every need. She sat there as he talked, silent tears in her eyes. She was being strong for us—as always. Kim remained frozen, her world crumbling before her. Up until now (to my knowledge), Dad had only hurt me. Now, he was tearing apart everyone I loved. *How could he be so selfish?*

I asked Mom if she knew the woman and she nodded her head. When I found out who it was, I freaked out.

Hyperventilating and screaming, I ran into the bathroom and threw up, my heart crushing in two. My mom had been betrayed by her husband and her best friend! And I knew my half-sister!

I pictured her watching Kim and me from afar. I felt her loneliness. She probably thought our lives were perfect. She probably wondered what was wrong with her, why he had never acknowledged her. Every day I wondered what was wrong with me. I knew he loved me but… images, careless words, the slamming of doors flashed through my mind.

"If you don't change your attitude, I'm sending you off to a boarding school. You won't be talking to your mom or Kim every day, either. You can come home twice a year…" He was sitting in his chair at the kitchen table when he told me this. I was nine. He never sent me away, but so many seeds of rejection and despair were planted. He "threw me out of his life" four other major times, saying he was done with me, that I was no longer welcome in *his* house, etc. Usually it was because I disagreed with him and he was "tired of my mouth." Other times, he was just in a mood. Sometimes, he apologized the next day. Other times, it took months. Each time I forgave him.

Only someone who has experienced this type of emotional and verbal abuse can comprehend the pain. But the pain wasn't the biggest problem. It was the constant worrying, the self-doubt, and fear of abandonment that would cost me the most.

I didn't want to forgive him this time. I also didn't want to feel bad for him. But I did. I knew he was hurting too, and *somehow* I knew what it was like to do something you couldn't take back. I also knew that if my Mom had forgiven him that I had to, too. She deserved that.

My new sister, Holly, was the blessing in the midst. We were all determined—and eager—to make our new family work. No one did everything perfectly in this scenario, and if I had to do it again, I would do many things differently. But after falling in love with my new sister and watching my mom embrace her, when he, consumed by guilt, decided to put my mom, Kim and me—to put it nicely—"on the back burner," I knew I couldn't take his kind of love any longer.

At night, I'd lie awake for hours, trembling, feeling nothing. When I'd finally fall asleep, I'd dream of him stabbing me in the heart. I'd wake up ice cold and sweating. I couldn't breathe. I became petrified that I was going to hurt people like he was doing. (This was due to things he had told me throughout my life.) Because of all this, I went to a psychiatrist. I was prescribed medication for depression and anxiety, and given sleeping pills. I stopped taking the sleeping pills after only a few days. I wanted to sleep, not be dead to the world. (I am not suggesting that anyone take themselves off medication. I'm merely sharing what I did.)

Surprisingly, I opened up about the eating disorder. As I answered her questions, in a messed up way, it finally made sense. She also helped me understand where my fears were coming from. How I felt and responded to people and situations went back a long way. All of them, in one way or another, had to do with my dad.

My dad loves me and never meant to hurt me. I've forgiven him with my whole heart, and don't blame him or anyone else for any of my problems. Circumstances, biological makeup, the way we process pain, generational curses, and many other things influence our decisions. But we are still the ones who make them.

People can only love or understand us to the extent that they love and understand themselves. When they haven't experienced God's love, or when what is right in their mind is based on the wrong they've experienced, they unintentionally share their faulty foundation with us.

When we don't deal with our insecurities, our fears, our pride, our lust, our self-satisfying, gratifying persona, or whatever else our issues may be, it's not only our lives that are affected. "Our story," whether good or bad, a mess or a masterpiece, is a chapter in someone else's book.

"You're not him," the psychiatrist told me.

She was right about that. However, she was wrong about this…

I remember it like it was yesterday. "I don't think you will need your medicine much longer, you are doing so much better," she smiled.

My insides froze. Better? I downed four beers at work and popped an anxiety pill before walking into her office. I couldn't even think about those band aids being taken away.

4

Moving On

I will instruct you and teach you in the way you should go; I will counsel you with my loving eye on you (Psalms 32:8 NIV).

I wasn't okay, but I wasn't giving up. I kept singing and acting, ditched the anxiety pills, and finally moved to LA. It was a dream come true.

About eight months later, both my sisters decided to move in with me. My mom had gotten a divorce and was living in Atlanta, which was about half way between where Kimber and Holly lived, so we met there. Mom helped us push, shove, and cram everything they owned into Kim's tiny car. She made us promise to be careful, cheered us on, and waved goodbye.

Driving through Texas, my two sisters asleep in the back, Mom's face in my heart, I pulled off to the side of the road. The sky looked so big and vast. All I could think of was how amazing God is. *If only my dad would…*

The three of us lived in my one-bedroom apartment in Hollywood. It was both wonderful and weird. We all had our own issues and ways of dealing with life. But one thing was for sure—we loved each other, and were so glad to be together.

Eventually, Holly went home. I wish she had stayed. I wish I could have done more. I wish a lot of things.

~ ~ ~ ~ ~ ~ ~

When I lived in NYC, I had studied acting at The Lee Strasberg Theater, Weist Barron, and HB Studios. I was good—but I still felt like I was winging it. When Kimber heard about The JoAnne Barron, DW Brown School in Santa Monica, she excitedly told me that I had to go there. It sounded great, but when she rattled off the A List actors who attended, the very ones who graced my favorite shows, I said, "I'm not as good as them."

Her response was, "Well, you can be the best with a bunch of wannabees, or you can be a small fish in the big pond and learn to swim." (She actually said it better than that.)

I knew she was right, so I called. You had to interview for the first six-week course—then get invited back, and it was a two-year program. Committing to anything for six weeks was barely comprehendible, but two years?

It was one of the best times of my life. It included everything I loved. Acting, psychology, crazy, committed people… Everyone was different—and I fit in perfectly. It's amazing being a part of, and in the midst of, so many dreams.

In addition to acting, Kim and I started singing together. We'd come home from our awesome church and Kim would sit down at the piano or pick up her guitar and I would sing. Hours would go by before we realized it. Afterwards we'd talk about how a three minute song can change your life and how far Christian music had come. Eventually, our conversations always rolled around to, "But what about people who don't go to church? What about all the people at bars listening to songs that identify with their problems, but just lead them to more problems? Why is there such a gap between the Christian and secular world? God meets people where they are and offers them something different. Why can't music do that?"

The piano woke me up the next morning. Kim was never up before me. "What are you doing?" I asked, walking into the living room.

Kim's eyes and fingers didn't leave the keys. "Go get one of your journals."

"What are you playing? I love it!"

"Shh don't talk. Just get one of your journals."

I started to ask which one, but remembered I wasn't supposed to talk. Before I opened my angel chest (which held half my life), I knew which one. "You're playing this!" I yelled, running down the hall.

"Hope on Hollywood Boulevard," was our first original song. We worked on it day and night for weeks. (Luckily for us, the ladies across the hall, also sisters, were in their 80's and hard of hearing.) By the end of the month, I had gone through all of my journals and pulled out everything song worthy. Kim was a machine, whipping up a melody a minute. We knew we were on to something, and with each second, got a little more excited.

The more we sang, the more we felt God's presence. I was also going on auditions. I loved acting, but the closer I got to God, the more I cared about what part I was playing. In other words, I was tired of auditioning for the blond bimbo and seductress roles. I wanted to make a difference.

And that's exactly what we were doing with our music. It had started with a conversation about us wishing there were songs that met you where you were, but left you with hope, and now we were writing them! Songs that were edgy enough for the secular world, but inspired you to believe in more. Songs for people who were struggling and looking for love and acceptance in all the wrong places. People who were fighting to get back up—people like you and me.

The more we sang, the more we believed that this was God's plan for us. After a lot of praying, we made a commitment to God and to each other, to devote the rest of our lives to pursuing a career in Christian music. We knew God had big plans for us.

I stopped acting and put all of my focus on our music. This was it. No more dreaming alone, I finally had a partner. One that I loved, admired, and was oh, so much fun! Plus, Kimber had always been popular, the best at everything. Everything she touched turned to gold. Combining forces with my sister was the winning combination.

Being sisters, best friends, and business partners, working, rehearsing and living together, things weren't always perfect, but *we* were right. Life was good.

After years of hard work, we were finally working with the majors. However, right after auditioning for Pamplin Music, alongside Sharenda Roam and Katy Hudson (now Katy Perry), who both signed with the label, Kim decided she was done with the Christian entertainment industry. It's true that it can be shadier than the secular world (mainly because you expect it to be better), but I always knew this. It was one of the reasons we were doing what we were doing. We were supposed to be a light in the darkness!

Anyway, that was her official reason for quitting. However, she saw in private what I managed to hide from everyone else, 90% of the time. I was a drinking a lot. Drinking had never been a problem, but when everything happened with our family, I started drinking to cover up the pain. Because it was something I had always done, it was an easy habit to abuse. The habit had become an addiction.

I recorded the songs we had written together by myself. I could be a solo artist… I had been one for years. The only difference was, now I knew what it was like to have a partner. I knew what it was like to share every prayer, every tear, every mishap, every milestone, to have someone kick you into gear when you were tired, encourage you when you were down, and make you laugh no matter what. When you've shared the thrill of anticipation, as well as the weight of carrying a dream that is bigger than you with someone—it's hard to go back to being alone.

One of my favorite pastors once said that most people quit right before their greatest breakthrough. I remember thinking how I would never do that. But that is exactly what I did. A few months after Kim pulled out, I gave up everything I had ever wanted, everything I had sacrificed for, everything I had ever believed in. *How could Kim have done this? Why did she wait until now? I had stopped acting. We were a team...*

I didn't follow any of the advice I share in this book. I did not take a good look at myself in the mirror. I did not dig deep. And though I prayed about "what to do," my emotional state made it hard to hear anything other than my pain. As mad as I was, as hurt as I was... I just missed my sister. And I was scared.

Instead of "waiting on the Lord," I took matters into my own hands and did what never works. I made not one, but many decisions, while going through a major transition (better known as hell). I moved across the country. I got engaged. I begged God to take away every dream He had ever given me. Just to let me be normal. Of course, I justified every decision so well, that no one ever questioned me. I almost believed myself. Almost.

Long story short, I got unengaged. I moved again, finally making it back to New York City.

It had been a long and hard road, but Kimber and I were friends again. I had a good job, was active in my church, did volunteer work regularly... People were always commenting on what a "light" I was. Yet most every night I cried (or drank) myself to sleep. I'd lie in bed holding my heart. I could literally feel it ripping apart. It hurt to dream. It hurt to remember. *Why did I give up? How did I come so far from who I was, who I was supposed to be?* Like an old cassette tape on repeat, my regrets played over and over in my mind.

There is nothing worse than knowing God has a huge call on your life and not pursuing it. Not only was I not pursuing it, I was doing everything I could to drown it out. Alcohol was my blanket. I drank to feel. I drank to numb the pain. I drank at least twenty beers a day for years. The only thing was, no matter how hard I tried, I couldn't drown out the dreams inside me. I also had no idea what to do with them.

I lived on a tightrope. With fear on one side, and faith on the other. I balanced very well, for a very long time. But balancing takes every bit of our energy—and it's one of the biggest distractions to our destiny.

Our struggles either strangle us or transform us. I was tired of choking. I had been tired of it for a long time. *But where to begin...*

I knew I had to stop drinking. It was going to take everything I had and then some. But I knew I could do it. Dealing with all the reasons of why I was where I was—that I wasn't so sure about.

Unlike the former food issue, there was no "voice" telling me to drink. There was no crazy desire or compulsion. I just didn't care. *I cared so much.*

5

Re-Discovering Me

Sometimes a God-dream is the only thing strong enough to lead you home.

I had tossed and turned for hours before finally falling into a deep sleep—

"You're the most positive person I know... the most positive person I know. But you've got to stop doing what you are doing. You have to do what you are afraid of doing, so I can use you. The plan I have for you is so big. Bigger than your wildest imagination, bigger than your dreams, bigger than anything you can comprehend. The plan I have for you is the only one that will fulfill you. You know this. And you want it too! But you've been hurt and you're scared. You've chosen to hide and cry and not truly live."

"You've got to stop doing what you are doing! You've got to start living so I can live through you. The Son will set you free. You've let Him touch you before, so get up once again. This time do it fully. I'm with you all the way. Wait and see! Just get up and do it again. Trust me. You've got to do what you are scared of doing.

Your life will become like Mine. You're the most positive person I know, the most positive person I know..."

I knew this dream was important and tried to wake myself up so I could get a pen and write it down. *"Stay still. Do not move. You will remember."* I lay there as still as I could, completely asleep and completely aware.

"My plan is so big. But you have to stop. Stop doing what you are doing. I need you. You're the most positive person I know. The most positive person I know...

The sun shining through the windows woke me. I remembered the dream fully. It made no sense. And it made perfect sense.

"You've been hurt and chosen to hide and cry and not truly live. You've got to stop doing what you are doing!" This was about drinking, obviously.

"The plan I have for you is so big. Bigger than your imagination, bigger than your dreams, bigger than anything you can comprehend." I always knew God had big plans for me. But I had messed up. It was too late...

"You've let Him touch you before. Do it again. But this time, do it fully. I'm with you all the way." God was referring to the eating disorder that controlled my life for so long. Jesus delivered me, but I didn't deal with the underlying issues of why I was self-sabotaging in the first place, so even though it never controlled me again, it was still a part of my life for years after.

"The plan I have for you is the only one that will fulfill you." As much as I craved love and wanted a soul mate, deep

down, I knew that nothing would fulfill me except *this thing* God was talking about. Even though I had no idea what the *thing* was, it had always been there. I had been searching for it my entire life. I had run from it, tried to leave it behind, but… it was what was keeping me alive.

I knew God was talking to me. I understood all of it. Except for the positive part. I was depressed. I was a mess. *Positive?* I had no idea why God would say that. Yet I knew the dream was from Him. I took it in. I treasured it. I wish I could say it changed my life. It should have. Maybe in the long run it did.

⸻ ⸻ ⸻ ⸻ ⸻ ⸻ ⸻

Throughout the next year, I sought to find myself more than I ever had. I dug deep. But this time, instead of being strong when I looked at my past, I let myself cry for the little girl who had held so much inside. I let myself feel the fear and the hurt, and all that wasn't right. It was as if I were standing above the situation apologizing to myself. I didn't put this together at the time, but I stood in the gap for everyone I needed apologies from and was able to let go.

I also read countless psychology books, listened to at least five sermons a week and attended two to three church services a week. I wrote, prayed, and cried. There was an absolute battle going on in my life (actually the battle was *for* my life), but for the first time in a long time, I had hope in the midst of my hopelessness.

However, when God gives you a revelation or speaks to you like He did in my dream, no matter how many good things you do, or how much improvement you make, if you don't completely surrender, it's bound to get worse. And it did. Even though God had spoken to me, even though I had almost died three times from alcohol poisoning, I had not completely stopped drinking.

There were days I didn't drink at all. There were days I drank less than I had in years. And then there were those when I drank more and more and more. I wasn't going to make it much longer. Something was changing—it's like there had been this cloud of protection over my head. I hadn't known it was there, but I could feel it slowly moving away. With it were opportunities to pursue the plan God created me for. An indescribable loneliness swept through me. And stayed.

~ ~ ~ ~ ~ ~ ~

Lent was around the corner, and some friends were discussing what they were giving up. I had never observed Lent, but "I should give up drinking" crossed my mind more than once. Since I had never fasted and hadn't gone a day without beer for over a decade, I decided seven days would be a good start. *One week. I can do this.*

Have you ever had a dream where you can literally feel the person with you? One that is so real that when you open your eyes you're disoriented? This was how I woke up on the first morning of Lent. I had been dreaming of my ex-fiancé. It wasn't just a reminiscing, "I miss you," dream. It was like he was in my soul. I felt his touch. This would have made a little more sense if we had just broken up, but it had been years. Yet my heart ached as much as the day I left. Even though I had closed my eyes to reality when I moved across the country and got engaged, I was very much in love. Whether right or wrong, I gave my whole heart, and when you do this, you never get it all back. Staying would have been catastrophic. But it didn't make leaving any easier.

Normally, I would have attempted to wash the dream away. But today was the first day of my seven day commitment not to drink. Surprisingly, instead of thinking "This sucks," the realization of, "So this is how it's going to be," moved through me.

On the second day, an incurable disease that God had healed me from in 1999 returned. Not only did this put me in great physical pain, the anguish was awful. *Why is this happening? Why would God do this to me?* flooded my heart. I answered my own questions with *God isn't doing this to me.* This was the devil. I did my best to ignore the "false evidence appearing real," and reminded myself that God does not take away healing. Within a few days I was fine, and have been ever since.

What I was healed from is not the point. The point is, that the devil will stop at nothing to make you believe that God doesn't care, that you are too far gone, that there is no way you can deal with your life without whatever crutch you are depending on. It's why the Bible calls him a thief and a liar who only comes to steal, kill, and destroy.

There was an attack on my heart, body, and soul, every single day of that week. It seemed God had deserted me, and I was in a battle with the devil, all by myself. But it was a battle I was determined to win. By the fifth day, I felt pretty good. *Maybe I'll just be done...* However, when day seven arrived, I was so proud of myself that I rewarded myself with a beer.

I liked having just a couple drinks a day. But all of the reasons I drank so much in the first place were still there. It wasn't long before I was drinking morning, noon, and night. Making sure no one knew was a full time job. By Friday, it took every ounce of willpower I had to hold it together. I'd stumble home, climb my five flights of stairs and fall into bed. When I fell into bed on this particular Friday, I knew I was in trouble. I was shaking all over. My body was ice cold but I was hot as fire. Every part of my body ached. I had to hold the walls for balance to get to the bathroom. My blood pressure was 210 over 160 and climbing. I knew I needed to go to the hospital, but I honestly didn't think I'd make it out the door.

"God, I am so sorry." My words sounded empty, even to me. The dream God gave me played through my mind. Cut through my heart. I didn't even know what God's plan was, yet it burned inside me. I had to change or I was going to die, in more ways than one. I made a promise to God that I'd do whatever He said, just to use me.

On Sunday, I dragged myself to church. I barely made it through the service. The next morning, July 4th, still shaking, I went to an AA meeting. (I had gone to them sporadically over the last year. I never talked. Just listened.) *I had to be done drinking. I just had to be.*

It was amazingly weird how much better I felt the next day. It's like nothing had happened. And unlike the first time I stopped drinking, something special happened each day that week—including what is now *Believe*. Before I share this with you, let me backtrack—

A few weeks prior to this, I was deep in thought while walking across a busy street in NYC. This guy whisked me out of the way, as a car flew by almost hitting me. After I caught my breath, we started talking and he walked me to my destination. Almost getting hit by a car was far from my mind, because we were having the most meaningful conversation I had had in years.

Before parting, he looked at me and said, "You should write your dreams down." I agreed that I should, and commented that a few of my best songs had come from dreams. He smiled and made me promise that I'd write them down. The whole experience left me standing at the corner of 14th Street and Park Avenue, in awe.

Unfortunately, we let life evaporate our awe moments and carry on as usual. *Please don't do this.*

Back to July

I went to sleep on July 7th thanking God for my life. Not only was I sober, the hope welling inside me was nothing short of a miracle.

I was having the best dream. Even in my sleep, I knew I was supposed to write it down, but I didn't want to wake up. The dream was hopeful and happy but something bad was going to happen. *"Write this down."* I buried my head into the pillow. *"You need to write this down."* The voice was getting louder. *"Write this down!"* I'll do it in the morning, I thought. *"That's not what you said you were going to do."* Whoa! Now I was awake! I sat straight up in bed and switched on the light. It was 3:13. I picked up a pen, opened my journal, and started writing.

I knew when I was "done," and fell right back to sleep. The next morning, I was wide awake. I only remembered about three minutes of the dream, yet I had written nearly twenty-five pages. I ran to work, my heart beating a little faster. My ten-hour waitress shift wasn't as bad as usual—while I was taking orders, I was also scribbling down dialogue and characters that kept coming to me. A few days later, I was walking across my living room floor when it hit me. I was writing a book for middle graders. And it was good! Instantly I heard, *"What are you going to do with it? You're wasting your time. You already work fifty hours a week, you're exhausting yourself for nothing. You don't know anything about writing a book. It will be just like your music. You will get your heart broken all over again. You can't take that."* I knew this voice well. I had heard it my entire life. It was louder now. It also sounded… desperate. Fearful. No longer did I think this voice was just an icky feeling. This was the voice of the enemy.

And then, almost like a lightning bolt cutting through, I heard, "JUST WRITE." *God's voice.* So strong. Adamant. So—non-negotiable.

For the first time in my life, I did exactly what God said. I didn't question the how, when or what. I didn't try to come up with answers to all of the realistic points the enemy had brought up. I just wrote. I also slept with my journal and pen right beside me. In addition to *Believe*, God was giving me visions of my future.

I wrote the entire book in less than two months, while working a full time job. And when it was finished—I was lost. I've experienced zillions of lows in my lifetime, but this low was on a whole other level. I now know this is what writers refer to as "post project depression." Similar to post-partum, it is very real and very common. All I knew then was that my flying carpet of energy had been swooped out from under me. I sat in Bryant Park, staring at a world going on without me. I felt numb. Disconnected from life, from myself, from God... *Now what?*

When people look at others and think, "I can't believe they—" How could they—?" I get it. It is heartbreaking when people "go back" after a breakthrough. I also understand. It is our human nature to go back to what we know.

For the flesh desires what is contrary to the Spirit, and the Spirit what is contrary to the flesh. They are in conflict with each other, so that you are not to do whatever you want (Galatians 5:17 NIV).

I drank thirty beers a day for the rest of the week. I won't go into the details, but it was worse than it had been in July. I lay in bed wanting to cry out to God, but there were no more tears. Just guilt and shame. Why had I done this? What was wrong with me? Was I going to die? I pictured my Mom. I couldn't do this to her. I had to make everything up to her.

The plans God had for me swam through my heart. I saw the faces of kids and teens that were going to be changed because of my testimony. Adults that would believe again... there were so many people... so many things... God had trusted me. What if I lived, but God found someone else to carry out the plan He had for me? *God please don't do this. I don't want to live without You. I want to be the me you created! But I'm scared. I'm so scared. I want to trust You! It makes no sense not to. You're the only One who has never left me.*

Why couldn't I trust Him? I wanted to with all my heart but... something was in the way. Something stronger than me. Something that was pulling me under each time I tried. *Please don't give up on me. Please use me. I don't deserve it, but...* While I was saying all this in my head, a voice rose inside of me. Almost as if it were fighting through the layers of mess to be heard, *"I deserve it."*

It was the same voice that told me I didn't belong in Kentucky. It was the same voice that gave me the strength to hold my head up as I walked through the corridors of high school being mocked. It was the voice that enabled me to walk away from people who held my hopes and dreams in one hand, and ulterior motives in the other. It was the voice of hope I had held onto for so long. I had stopped listening—but it had not let me go. The real me was making a demand on the me I had become.

God chose me for big things. I had messed them up, ridiculously and horrifically. But I was still breathing, and as long as we are still breathing there is hope. I forced myself out of bed. I needed to eat. I made it to the kitchen, but couldn't swallow food. I sank down to the floor and started praying.

Someone was laughing. At first I thought it was the neighbors, but this wasn't happy laugher. It was hollow and... I pulled myself up. A heaviness filled the room. Something was happening—I wasn't alone. Though I couldn't see their faces or hear their voice in a physical sense, something or someone was to the left of me, and someone was on the right. "God? Are you here?" Jesus was to my right, but was moving farther and farther away. I felt His sadness. *"After all I did? After everything I showed you?"* A deep "I told you so" laugh came from the left.

For years, I had begged, cried, and pleaded for God to help me. But I had never done, what I now know, we are authorized by Christ to do. "Devil get away from me! Leave me alone. Leave me alone! In Jesus' Name! You can't have me anymore! Go back to hell where you belong!" Suddenly, I was on my feet, swiping at the air, demanding that he leave me alone. I kept screaming and he kept laughing. I shouted out every scripture I could think of. "God please don't leave me. I want Your plan. I want it so bad. I want to live. I want to truly live! Please forgive me." The devil's laughter wasn't as loud—but he refused to let go of me. That is, until he heard the voice that saves us all. *"That's it. Leave her alone!"* Instantly the room was different. The air was clear. I sat down on the floor, thanking and praising God.

Jesus stayed with me. He spoke to me. He assured me everything God had shown me would happen. But it was going to take time. And it was going to be hard. I remember lots of images that would later make sense. *"There is a lot against... Just Believe. Don't stop believing."*

The Bible tells us that Jesus died for our sins on the cross. But no matter how many times we read about it and see it portrayed on film and TV, it's still surreal. I stood in the middle of my living room on 29th Street and Madison Avenue and witnessed Jesus fighting for my life. He released me from the enemy's grip. There would be no more broken promises. No more drinking. Whatever it took. Whatever He wanted. For the rest of my life, I was His.

The next few weeks (minutes, days and hours) were not easy. Circumstances (like being stranded in my alcohol ridden apartment for days when Hurricane Irene, the worst storm to hit NYC since 1972, shut down the whole city, for example), fears, doubts, habits—almost everything tempted me to drink. But the part of me that held on when I lay in bed dying, spoke up every time. The Holy Spirit was becoming my friend. He was with me every second. He was loving. He was authoritative. He even made me laugh a few times with the way He would say, "Don't you dare!" Each day I grew stronger. The me I had almost given up on, the me I had yet to become was emerging. I was learning to live again. To breathe again. I had hope! God had not taken away His purpose and His plan for me. He had saved me for it.

It took three months for all hell to break loose.

6

Spiritual Warfare

Beloved, do not be surprised at the fiery trial when it comes upon you to test you, as though something strange were happening to you. But rejoice insofar as you share Christ's sufferings, that you may also rejoice and be glad when His glory is revealed (1 Peter 4:12–13 ESV).

Prior to my sobriety, there had been a fire in my apartment building. With firefighters coming in and out, the doors were open for long periods of times. And now—the building was blazing with rats. It was horrid. I'd hide my head under the covers, trying to block out the sound of rats running rampant in the walls and ceilings. I'd remind myself that I was sober… God had trusted me with a book to write…

There was no way around it. I had to move out of my first real apartment in NYC. Looking for an apartment in New York is harder than looking for a job, but after weeks of searching, I saw an ad from an older woman who was renting out a small bedroom in her luxurious apartment. The place looked like a hotel and was over my budget, but I had always loved older people. *Maybe she'll really like me and offer to lower the price.* With a combination of desperation and hopefulness, I gave her a call.

Her name was the same as one of the characters in my book! And not just *a* character, but an earth-angel type character. Equally amazing, I had never heard of the name before, it had just "come to me" while writing. I called my mom on the way to the apartment, "Can you believe this?"

Mom was more than ready for my life to get easier, and was really excited. But when I mentioned the measurements of the room she said, "That's about the size of our bathroom."

"I don't care how small it is, all I need is a desk and file cabinets."

"File cabinets?" Mom laughed. "You will be lucky if you can fit a bed in there."

As soon as the woman opened the door, she seemed to read my mind. She answered my questions before I asked them. She even offered to lower the rent for me! "Can we talk for a minute?" she asked. I was eager to see the room but smiled and sat down at the dining room table with her.

This was nothing like the usual "what do you think of the apartment" conversation. She told me about her family. Her lost love. The betrayal of her sister and her first husband. I found it a little odd, but I'm used to people opening up to me so I didn't put too much into it. She also wanted to know everything about me. What was I passionate about? What kept me going? She wanted to know about my dreams, if my family supported me, were my parents together, how long had I lived on my own, had I struggled, etc. I rarely open up about these things, but I did that day. She seemed to "get me." Which I have to admit, felt really good.

My mom was right. The room I'd be staying in was tiny. But there was a day bed (I used to beg my parents for a day bed!), a long desk—and file cabinets. I called Kimber the minute I left and told her everything. "What did you say the address was?" she asked excitedly. I took the lease out of my purse and read it to her. "This is so your time!" she exclaimed.

"What?" I asked, already over the top with all the "signs."

"That's the address of ----------!" (The major publishing company I had just sent my manuscript to.)

The publishing company was on the other side of the city, but the street numbers were the same. "This is so God I don't even need to pray about it!"

~ ~ ~ ~ ~ ~ ~

I moved in on a beautiful day. The woman was gone for the weekend, which was good, because it gave me some space to get unpacked. I expected to be excited, but something was bothering me. Something felt weird. Off. "Of course you feel weird," I told myself. In the last three months I had stopped drinking, wrote a book, dealt with a fire, rats, no hot water, and for the last twelve hours I'd been running up and down five flights of stairs moving everything I owned. Who wouldn't feel weird?! *That had to be it.* I pushed the feeling aside. Besides, I only had a few more hours to unpack before I had to book it to the airport. In less than fifteen hours, I was going to be with my sister.

"How was the first night at your new place?" Kimber asked, as soon as I got off the plane.

"I slept funny," I said, not caring at the moment.

She threw my bag in the car. "What do you mean?"

"I'm not sure."

Kim looked at me. "You've been through a lot. New bed, new place."

I had been a spokesperson for an international company for years and virtually lived in hotels for seven months out of the year. I could sleep anywhere. "Yeah," I agreed, knowing that wasn't it. "So tell me everything," I said, wanting to cherish every second we had together. We had so much fun that I barely thought about the weird feeling in my gut.

~ ~ ~ ~ ~ ~ ~

The icky feeling was there as soon as I got off the plane. The closer I got to the apartment the worse it got. *Please don't let her be home.* What was wrong with me? I liked this woman. I chalked it up to being tired and reminded myself of all the "signs." I hadn't even asked for her to lower the rent, the room had everything I needed…

It was after midnight by the time the taxi dropped me off, yet she was up vacuuming. When I came home from work the next day, she was in my room. My stomach tightened. This was not okay! But because of my "respecting elders" upbringing, I didn't say anything.

Even though our agreement stated that I was renting the apartment, she made it clear that she wanted me in my room. Anytime I came out of my room, she was right there. One day, she told me that the girl who used to rent my room had gone crazy. She had tried to help, but "in the end drove her to the psych ward." The story was tragic. But the way she told it, it was like she was proud.

Weird things started to happen. She'd leave the house on the weekends, yet music would come from her room throughout the night. I'd sit in the living room and feel like I was being watched. I'd open my Bible and fall asleep. When I woke up and turned on the lights, they'd shake.

I won't go into all the details, but I was hiding in the bedroom one afternoon thinking about how this woman was NOT the angel from my book, when I heard a taunting voice laughing. *"It's all a lie. The visions you think were from God, the dream, it's all been a joke."* A horrible fear rose inside me. I was shaking, frozen, and nauseated all at once. My insides were crushing and I couldn't breathe. Instantly, I heard God say, *"Get out. Get out of this house. Now!"*

God has told me many things in my life. He told me to stop drinking for years before I did. He told me not to date certain people, and to break up with other ones' way before I did. He told me what to do, but let me go around and around the mountain. I had never heard Him sound like this.

I grabbed a coat and ran out into the freezing city. I moved through the streets, oblivious to the snow and sleet pouring from the sky. "God what is going on?" All of a sudden, I remembered a sermon I had heard last year. My pastor had quoted John Wesley saying, "God is limited by our prayer life—He can do nothing for humanity unless someone asks Him." And then I remembered myself saying, "This apartment is so perfect I don't even have to pray about it." *Oh my gosh.*

I waited until I knew the woman would be gone before I went back. I immediately opened my Bible—it landed on Ephesians 6:12. I hadn't read Ephesians in years, did not have it bookmarked, yet there it was. *"For our struggle is not against flesh and blood, but against the rulers, against the authorities, against the powers of this dark world and against the spiritual forces of evil in the heavenly realms."* Though I didn't fully understand this, I knew it applied to the situation I was in.

I have a dear friend in the Bronx who is a mature and powerful believer. I called and asked if we could talk. Andréa happened to be on her way to the city. We met that night, and I filled her in on what was happening. "And I'm sleeping funny. I haven't had one dream since I've been there, but something's going on in my sleep."

Andréa looked at me. "How's your job?"

I was hoping she wouldn't ask. "I got fired."

"You got fired?" she asked, shocked. "Why?"

I shrugged. "No reason."

"When did that happen?"

"A couple days after I moved in."

"How's your writing?" she asked calmly.

Out of everything, this confused and upset me the most. "I don't know what's wrong. I sit down to write and everything is foggy. I can't concentrate. Writing is when I feel the closest to God and…"

"Do you not know anything about spiritual warfare?" She moved me out the next night and took me to her apartment in the Bronx.

Having no real understanding of spiritual warfare could have cost me my life. (Why I didn't, after being a Christian for most of my life, is something we will discuss in chapter eleven.) The apartment situation was a trap. A setup from the enemy that was meant to take me down for good. Instead, it drove me to the Bible. It made me stronger, wiser, and more aware of the enemy's tactics. It also made me extremely grateful for friends like Andréa.

Meanwhile, it was three months into my sobriety—I had lost my job, half of my savings, was living in the Bronx, and my face, which had broken out in crazy acne (about the time I moved in), was worse. Now, I've had my fair share of "breakouts caused by stress," but what was happening to my face, wasn't normal. After seeing my mom at Christmas she agreed that something was wrong and urged me to go to the doctor.

"I'll have to run a few tests," said the doctor. "But it looks like bedbugs."

My mind flashed to a card the woman had taped to my bedroom door. "Welcome Home! Hope you sleep like a bug in a rug."

"Yep. Bedbug bites," stated the doctor.

If this book just fell out of your hands, I understand.

I spent hours going through everything I owned, my heart pounding. Pictures, books, clothes, curtains, pillows—in the end, I threw away everything. It took over a year for my face to heal. As bad as all this was, I knew what was happening. The devil was scared. He knew what I was capable of when I was drinking. Now that I was free, I was completely available for the plan God had for me.

There were many days when I had to close my eyes to remember, but I held on to the words and visions God had given me with everything I had, and refused to do anything other than move forward. I had no time to think about the past—I was too busy honoring everything God was telling me to do now. I knew if I followed His lead and refused to doubt, that the dreams He blessed me with would become realities.

Within the next five years, I wrote three books for children, countless songs and messages for kids, teens, and adults, over one hundred articles for *The Daily Positive*, and One Church LA (a mega church in Los Angeles pastored by Touré Roberts and Sarah Jakes Roberts), and created a television series for teens that can bridge the gap between the religious and secular industries. I speak at youth conventions, women's events, churches…

It has not been smooth sailing—at all. I make daily decisions that are in complete contrast to what my feelings say I need. I've written when my heart was breaking, worked jobs I hated, and have been let down and disappointed too many times to count. I'm sure you have similar stories. All we can control is what we do with that. Making—and then keeping that promise to God, "I'll do whatever You say, just use me," changed my life. But it was just the beginning.

Whether God delivers us, supernaturally heals us, or whether we make a decision to say "no more" to whatever is in our way, we have to do our part. The "I have to have it now" persona has to go. We have to live by faith versus feelings. We can't allow disappointment to derail, unravel, and undo us. We have to be aware of distractions (both the good and the bad ones), trying to send us on detours.

I changed my story by incorporating everything I share in this book into my life. The tools we need to conquer addictions, to overcome depression, to change the way we think and speak, and to live life to our highest potential are intricately related. Therefore, the strategies we discuss in one chapter, can, and should, be used in all other "chapters" of our lives.

Having an intimate relationship with our Maker, as well as understanding ourselves, our patterns and tendencies, is what enables us to rise above, overcome, and walk in victory.

Michelangelo once said that "Every block of stone has a statue inside it and it is the task of the sculptor to discover it."

The real you is waiting to be revealed.

7

All Is Not Lost

Ask and it will be given to you; seek and you will find; knock and the door will be opened to you (Matthew 7:7 NIV).

There is a moment in every good movie where it looks like "All is lost." From our view, our favorite characters are going down. All odds are against them. Everyone they love has turned on them. Every part of their circumstance says, "It's over." We sit on the edge of our seats, holding our breath, our heart racing. We beg them not to make the wrong decision. We know if they keep believing—if they just hold on a little longer, help is on the way. We know things will get better.

Sometimes we fight for the person on the screen a lot more than we fight for ourselves.

God is the creator of our story. He knows the beginning, middle, and end. However, by giving us free will, He puts us in the director's chair. And "stories" only work when the director's vision is in line with the Creator's. For example...

In quick lightning flashes, God gave me the vision for the television series for teens that I mentioned. I saw every character clearly. They had big dreams and real problems. They were beautiful, talented, dynamic, and complex. I watched them make mistakes, fall in and out of love, make friends with their enemies and enemies out of friends. I saw them falling, yet never giving up. There was a lot of drama and tears. Music that both broke and healed your heart. It wasn't religious, but there was an underlying essence of hope running through everything. God was there. I know the impact this series will have if it stays in its original form.

However, if I were to sell this series to you, I'd have to walk away. If you had your own brilliant ideas and decided to re-write it, there would be nothing I could do. If you had questions or wanted my help, you'd have to call me and ask. If you took it in a different direction, then realized you'd ruined the whole thing—if you messed it up to the extent that you were embarrassed and ashamed—that's when I would want you to call me the most! I could tell you why it wasn't working because I created it. But if you didn't call, I couldn't help. Because there would be a legal contract that separated me from my initial creation, it would literally be "in your hands."

Sounds a lot like our relationship with God. When we don't communicate with our Creator, we make decisions that are contrary to who we truly are. We get involved with the wrong people. We get so far from God's plan for our lives, that we forget there ever was one. As a matter of fact, we want to forget. We do our best "not to think." But there are those moments. Those moments when we *know*. When nothing we do, not even the things that bring us great joy, can drown out that still small voice saying, "There's more."

Digging Deep

One of the best ways to find that "more" is by journaling. In a sense, I wrote myself well. Writing keeps us accountable. It shows us what is wrong, what needs changing. It reveals who we are and who we want to be, and if we look close enough, it shows us what is in the way of becoming that person.

Writing is Matthew 7:7 in action. *Ask and it will be given to you; seek and you will find; knock and the door will be opened.* Often, I'll ask God questions as I write and all of a sudden stop—for I've just written the answer. Other times, my pen flies across the page with answers that I had no conscious awareness of before I started writing.

Through journaling we get to know our true selves. We recognize our problems and patterns. However, knowing what needs to be done and not making those changes is like looking in the mirror and two minutes later not knowing what you look like. (See James 1: 23–24.)

One day, I decided I had been "looking in the mirror then running out the door" for too long. It was time to get serious. I sat down at the kitchen table on a snowy Saturday morning, and wrote down every single thing I was mad about, hated, and regretted in my life. Seven pages back and front. I planned on writing what I liked about my life too, but by the time I was done, I was physically and mentally exhausted, my fingers ached from writing, my nose was raw from using napkins to blow it, and I had to run out the door to catch a bus so I could get to the job I hated on time.

Making the list took courage. Getting to work on time was responsible. Neither was going to change anything. I had come this far many times—only to move full speed ahead in the wrong direction.

A lot of important details get pushed to the side when we're moving full speed ahead.

> More often than we'd like to believe,
> the addictions, the bad relationships,
> and every other problem we have,
> are our insides screaming,
> "Deal with me!"

We make our list. We scratch the surface of our lives. Sometimes we go deeper, and we're honest with ourselves about the mess we're in. But we're not completely honest. We dig just far enough to make ourselves—and a few of our loved ones— believe "we've got this."

Digging deep and dealing with my backstory was the key to changing my story. Needing a key signifies that something is locked. Without the key, we can't get in. The key to breaking the chains of addiction, re-training our brains, recognizing the power in our words and thoughts, understanding spiritual warfare, conquering depression, and unlocking our destiny, is heavy. I couldn't have held that key without holding God's hand.

Say a prayer. Take a breath. Write down all the things that aren't working in your life. Include the things you regret, and the things that need changing.

The one thing you don't want to write down holds the key to your breakthrough.

The Backstory

As a writer, people frequently ask, "How do you know what your characters are going to say?" The truth is, I have no idea what they will say. Not until I know their backstory. The backstory is everything that happens before the book or script begins.

Where did they grow up? Do they have brothers and sisters? Are their parents still together? Do they even know their parents? Do they date? Have they been married, abused, or cheated on? Do they believe in God? If so, what do they believe? Do they drink, smoke, or do drugs? If so, do they do this when they are happy, sad, need to relax, or just because? What do they do when nobody's watching? What do they want to do? What are their secrets? What do they regret? What are they scared of? Do they run away or stay and fight? Why do they run away? What makes them fight?

Not only do I have to know the trials, tribulations and triumphs they've faced, I also have to know how they've dealt with them. This is their backstory. It's what motivates their actions.

When I first started writing, if a line of dialogue wasn't working, I'd try to fix it. I'd try it a million different ways and it still wouldn't sound right. I finally realized that the problem wasn't with the dialogue, it was with my not knowing the character well enough.

When we don't know ourselves well enough, when we are afraid to dig deep, or worse, don't think it's important to our "now," we get a lot of lines wrong. We get ourselves in "scenes" that have nothing to do with God's original plan for our lives. Other times, we avoid and/or cut scenes that are absolutely supposed to be in our life.

> If you don't learn from the battle behind you,
> you won't see the one in front of you.

There is a backstory behind every problem we have, and every decision we make. Without dealing with them, we can choose the wrong partners, jobs, conversations, and lifestyles. We often swap one bad habit for another, trade addictions, and become defensive, manipulative, and controlling. We "move forward," leaving a part of us behind. We by-pass destiny altering opportunities and avoid relationships that cause us "to think." Something is always in our way. And that something, at least in part, is ourself.

Digging deep is not easy. It is the way through. But it has to be done with the right objective.

The Objective

"It's all about your objective," is one of the first things you learn in acting class. You can have ten actors rehearsing the same scene but depending on their objective (what they want), the scene will play differently with each actor.

Whether you are analyzing your own life or working through a relationship, you need to remind yourself why you are "digging deep." It is not to beat up yourself or anyone else. It is not to rehash or to replay mistakes, to justify your behavior, or to prove "everything is fine." It is to help you better understand yourself, your relationships, your habits, and patterns, so you can live a victorious life.

The objective is to turn every bit of pain into purpose. To never again make decisions based on fears, doubts or insecurities. To be done with self-sabotaging, and instead be your greatest confidante and cheerleader. To never again be satisfied with "status quo" living. To walk in truth, dignity, confidence, and righteousness. For your relationships to be real, authentic, meaningful, and based on truth. To listen intently with the desire to understand. To be slow to anger. To never judge. To love unswervingly. To give your all. To never stop dreaming, hoping and believing. The best is yet to come.

If you don't want history to repeat itself—deal with your backstory. If you say, "That's not the problem, it's…" Deal with your backstory. I promise it is affecting you.

Take back out your list and revisit the hard questions. If "I'm mad because I lash out," is on your list, ask yourself *why* you lash out. For each answer, ask "why." After you've gotten to the bottom of the whys, ask yourself questions such as: "When do I do this? When did I start doing this? Are there certain situations when this is more prone to happen? Do certain people trigger this?" If yes, then ask "why?"

Until you understand why you call the guy who abuses you, why you cheat, why you avoid certain conversations, why you have to completely exhaust yourself in order to relax, why you tell lies, are defensive, controlling, scared, spend money you don't have, and eat and drink too much... Well, even if you stop the behavior, the "why" will find another area of your life to rear its ugly head.

Before we move on, I want to touch on regrets. Because if your list is anything like mine was, it's probably full of them. Regrets are like puzzles with lots of pieces. Some of the pieces we can change, but unfortunately we usually focus on the parts we can't. I'm going to share a ridiculously true story with you to better explain what I mean.

I had been very interested in someone for over two years. He was in the public eye and not easily accessible, but my gut said "he might be the one." When he finally asked me out, it was during the worst time of my life. Nevertheless, we had a great time. It was like we had known each other forever.

The next time we saw each other was at an important event. As soon as he saw me, he invited me to sit with him and his friends. I had been drinking and didn't want him to know, so instead of joining him, I avoided him all night. Because of where we both were in our lives, I never had that chance again.

As you can imagine, ruining the opportunity that I had prayed for and believed in, was at the top of my list of regrets. The scenario played itself over and over in my head for a decade. But until I sat down at the kitchen table that day, I never made myself deal with the root of the regret. "Ruining my opportunity" was the result of my drinking too much.

I couldn't get that opportunity back—but by dealing with the "why," I could make sure alcohol was never the cause of my losing another one.

Digging deep is difficult. It takes everything you've got and then some. But "the closer you draw to God the closer He draws to you," is not just a slogan. The more you uncover your wounds, the more you will discover that Jesus is a friend like no other. He opens our eyes of understanding and entrusts us with insights and revelations that give us both the wisdom and courage to change.

Show me your ways, LORD, teach me your paths (Psalm 25:4 NIV).

8

Choosing to Change

Don't wait until the pain outweighs the pleasure to change.

You can lose five pounds before your high school reunion, your wedding, or your date on Friday night. You can stop drinking for ten days, just to prove you can. You can live on a budget—for a week. As long as we know there is an ending date, most of us can willpower our way through anything. Events, people, pride—anything can be the catalyst for change. But what happens when the event is over and the people you want to impress aren't around? What happens when you are by yourself?

Tim Storey, world renowned Pastor and Life Advisor, says that for change to last, "you have to get sick and tired of being sick and tired." That played in my heart and head for many years before I finally took the steps to truly turn my life around.

Why do we wait? What are we afraid of?
What makes change so intimidating?

If "because it takes forever" is the first thing that comes to mind, you are not alone. We have a microwave mentality. We like quick fixes. And if we are going to put the time in, we want to get it right the first time! None of these qualities gel well with change.

Change is hard because we hold on to the things we ask God to take away. We get comfortable in our problem. We complain that things need to change, yet keep putting up with the way things are. When it comes to relationships, sometimes we get so get so used to complaining, we don't see things have changed. For instance, one of the girls in my Bible study asked us to pray for a situation between her and one of her co-workers. It was so bad that even though she loved her job, she was ready to leave. One day, she stood up and gave a praise report. Then she immediately apologized for not giving it sooner. Things had been better for a long time, but she hadn't realized it because she was holding on to the hurt, the memory of how it used to be. It took something drastic for her to see that the problem was now her.

Our brokenness, our back-stories, our need for control hinders our perception. Change requires that we get new glasses. We have to see clearly to know what really needs changing.

On a deeper level, change is terrifying
because it requires trust.

At any point in my life, if you would have asked if I trusted God I would have said "Yes!" and I would have meant it. However, the decisions I made and the ones I didn't make told another story. When I dug deep enough, the reason I didn't want to stop drinking... I was scared. As much as I wanted to—as much as I said and thought I did, I didn't truly believe God still had a plan for me.

Where there is no revelation, people cast off restraint (Proverbs 29:18 NLT). When people do not accept divine guidance, they run wild (KLV). Where there is no vision, my people perish (NIV). It doesn't matter which translation of the Bible you read, the bottom line is the same. You have to be able to see past yourself and your circumstance, to see God's plan for your life.

Of course, circumstances matter. But it is the regrets, guilt, shame, and the "what if's" that hold us hostage. It is the words, hurts, anger, fear, wrong ideas, and false truths that have been planted inside us that have taken root and taken over, that keep us from moving forward.

We have to trust that we can change our story. That our tears haven't been in vain. That all is not lost. That God can and will use everything for our good. We have to believe that when God says, *"For I know the plans I have for you, plans to prosper you and not to harm you, plans to give you hope and a future"* (see Jeremiah 29:11), that He is talking about us. I didn't believe that. I said I did. I thought I did! But the reality is I relied on Miller Lite.

The devil works hard to manipulate our minds. Refusing to deal with our backstory, or covering it up and denying we have one, makes us vulnerable. We have to let go of the lies we've believed, and the ones we've lived in. We have to say goodbye to our fake security blankets. The only thing they protect us from is the truth—God loves us unconditionally. He hates to see us hurting and will never give up on us.

Close your eyes and picture yourself free from everything on your list. No more hiding, looking over your shoulder, pretending to be okay. You are confident, mature, worthy of respect. People look up to you because you set an example. They learn from you. You help them break free from the chains that kept you in bondage. Visioning this helps you endure the sleepless nights, the tears, the shakes, the loneliness, the anxiety, and all the other countless feelings that come with change.

Feelings Have a Mission
Change Requires Vision

Feelings demand our attention and make us focus on what feels good. They whisper what we want to hear.

"It doesn't matter… He'll get a job eventually."

"Go ahead! Everyone does it."

"One more drink won't hurt."

"Have another piece of cake."

"So what? You deserve to be happy."

Feelings tune out the warning signs, and tell us that "everything will be fine." They talk us into believing we don't care. That this time will be different. That we won't be sorry. Feelings tell us we can handle the consequences—and they lie.

Remove Feelings from the Driver's Seat of Your Life

Pretending to be happy all the time and ignoring your feelings is not what I'm talking about. Your feelings deserve to be heard and need to be understood—but sometimes you have to tell them to shut-up.

"Do the action and the feeling will follow." This advice came from my acting teacher in regards to a scene I was having trouble with. The scene called for me to cry, and I hadn't cried in years. (Why I couldn't cry was something my backstory would later revel.) I was so hung up on the emotions the scene called for that I was ruining what was a perfect part for me. "Forget about the emotion and focus on what your character is doing," yelled my teacher. Little did I know this would be one of the key ingredients to "changing my story."

Feelings are rarely in alignment with change. And I can promise you that anyone who has conquered giants, defeated the odds, risen above the status quo, and is living at their highest potential, did not get there by allowing their feelings to call the shots.

Not allowing feelings to be the driving force in my decisions was the biggest (and hardest), change I made. Yet without making this change—nothing else would have changed.

Stay committed to changing. Do what you said you were going to do, regardless of how you feel. Regardless of whether anyone is watching. Over and over again.

Change is not a "one stop shop." It is a process of daily decisions. A determination to get things right, no matter how much time it takes. It takes discipline, commitment, courage, and tenacity—it takes changing the way you think.

9

Re-Train Your Brain

Do thoughts of what you should have said and should have done make you dizzy? Is your mind full of guilt and shame? Who do your thoughts say you are? What do they say you can do?

My thought life was the biggest source of my problems. What's interesting is that it was also one of my greatest strengths. Again, we have the tightrope scenario. The battle with faith and fear. What God says and what the world says, in constant controversy.

"*Why is truth so hard to find? World makes it easy, believing the lies. I'm trying and fighting, souls about to drown. Heart and head, a battleground.*" That is a verse from "Hold On," a song my sister and I wrote. When is the last time you questioned your thoughts, your truths? Why do you believe what you believe?

Just like sin becomes normal after we live in it long enough, we can live in a "thought lie" long enough that it becomes our truth. Again, we must dig deep. We have to uncover the lies, pick them up by the root, and replace them with God's truth.

An Aha Moment

After receiving a compliment, my dear friend Andréa responded with, "I receive that." Later, I asked what she meant. (I didn't mention that I thought it sounded weird!) She gave me a "sometimes you really surprise me" look. "Do you take in everything people say to you?" she asked. I guess she could tell by the look on my face that I did. "Why would you do that?"

Because I never thought not to. "What do you say if you don't like what someone says?" I questioned.

"If it's not in alignment with what God says about me, I say, 'No thanks, I don't think that's for me!'"

I stood there thinking of all the comments I had let sink into my heart. All the commentary I had heard about myself. Of course, I didn't believe half of it—but I received it. And I had been dragging it around like an overweight backpack. How different my life would have been, if I had just said, "Yeah, that's not for me," and kept on walking.

> Thoughts don't appear.
> They are developed.
> Some of them have been with us our entire lives, and they don't just go away because we want them to.

There were many times in my life, when I *thought* I was doing the right thing, but my thoughts were coming from a place of brokenness. Sometimes we know we are broken. Other times, we have no idea how broken we actually are. We think we're fine. The neighbors think we're fine. Our friends look up to us, everyone at church admires us, and the few people who might not agree... well, we stay away from them. We can live an okay, even good, life like this. Yet we will never fulfill all the plans God has for us.

> *"Test me, Lord, and try me, examine my heart and mind" (Psalm 26:2 NIV).*

The Brain, Heart, and Mind Connection

Hope deferred can seriously make our hearts sick. It's why we are told in Proverbs 4:23 to "Guard our heart, for above all else, it determines the course of our life." At the same time, Hebrews 3:15 warns us not to harden our hearts. The combination of protecting, yet not closing our hearts, is a journey within itself. And it's one we must take.

Our hearts don't just pump blood. They talk to our brain. *"For as he thinketh in his heart, so is he" (Proverbs 23:7 KJV).* When our hearts are heavy, we can't think straight. We wander through life, ponder on words that should have never been spoken, and revisit memories that should have never been made.

A heavy heart, as well as not dealing with—or even realizing—we have a backstory, keeps us from hearing correctly. As I shared earlier, I loved every second of acting school. I was like a sponge. I took everything in, was always taking notes, and eager to get feedback. However, one day while critiquing my performance my teacher stopped mid-sentence. "You are not listening to me!"

I could feel my chest breaking out in red dots. What was she talking about? I was looking her in the eyes, I was taking notes—I was holding on to her every breath.

"You are not listening to me," she said again. "You think you are, but you're not. At some point in your life, someone said a lot of hurtful things to you. You weren't allowed to defend yourself, so you put a wall up to protect yourself. It might have helped you then, and you might have needed to! But right now, it's hurting you because I'm trying to help you and you can't hear me."

I completely thought I was listening. Yet she was absolutely right.

Don't let another person's lies
become your truth.

There are a lot of misconceptions about God. (Having my own cost me dearly.) We quote our favorite scriptures without understanding the context. We believe what we've heard and have been told because it is easier to accept than to seek. Not I, nor anyone else, knows everything, but I do know this—if you are suffering because of things that were done to you in the name of love that were everything but, if you've been abused, manipulated, molested… none of this was God's plan, nor was it your fault.

There is a powerful scene in the movie *Good Will Hunting*, where Robin Williams's character tells Will (Matt Damon) that what happened to him was not his fault. Over and over he repeats, "It's not your fault. It's not your fault. It's not your fault." The scene ends with Will crying—a major breakthrough. The guilt and shame we put upon ourselves due to the pain others have caused, is never ending—until we truly give it to God.

In John 16:33, God warns us that in this world we will have trouble, but to take heart, because He has overcome the world. But for us to overcome, we have to be *"transformed by the renewing of our minds."* (See Romans 12:2.)

Think of your brain like a big house that's been trashed. You can go out and buy the most beautiful, exquisite, and expensive furniture in the world. You can have it delivered. The workers can bring it in for you. But if you haven't gotten rid of the old furniture, where are they going to put it?

> *"For you can't sew a patch of unshrunk cloth on an old garment. The patch will pull away from the garment, making the tear worse. Neither do men pour new wine into old wineskins. If they do, the skins will burst, the wine will run out, and the wineskins will be ruined. No, they pour new wine into the new wineskins, and both are preserved"* (Matthew 9:16–17 NIV).

Ask God to reveal the thoughts and mindsets that are in your way. Yes, "we have the mind of Christ" (see 1 Corinthians 2:16), but in my experience, it's buried under a lot of life!

Trade Thinking for Trusting

Growing up, I always had a story going on in my head. "How is this going to happen? What will happen if? What will I do if---?" I'd create "what if" scenarios based on my current circumstances and plan conversations accordingly. This works well when I'm working on a script, but not so much when it comes to life.

Philippians 4: 6-7 tells us not to be anxious about anything, but in every situation, by prayer and petition with thanksgiving, to present our requests to God. It goes on to say that the peace of God, that transcends all understanding, will guard our hearts and minds in Christ Jesus. Memorize this scripture. Study it. Tape it to your mirror, your refrigerator, your front door—embed it in your heart, mind, and soul.

One of the biggest parts of "re-training our brains" is learning to trust God to work things out, versus trying to figure them out. (If you like to be in control, if you are a "fixer" or a "worrier," this will take some extra work.) Even the disciples, who walked with Jesus daily, had trouble with trusting. In Luke 9:12 Jesus' disciples were concerned that they didn't have enough food for the crowds. In verse 15, Jesus looked toward Heaven and gave thanks, then broke the bread into pieces. Not only was there enough for everyone but there were also twelve baskets left over.

Things happen in the spiritual realm before they manifest in the temporal (physical) realm, in which we reside. By thanking God in advance for taking care of our daily concerns, as well as the seemingly "impossible" areas of our lives, potential problems can be taken care of in the spiritual realm. If this happens, we won't have to deal with the problem we've spent anxiety-ridden hours stressing over at all. And if the situation does manifest itself into our lives, we will be making decisions and responding from a place of peace, from having spent time in prayer.

As soon as you realize your mind is drifting into the "what am I going to do" mode, start thanking God for working everything out for your good. Take Philippians 4:8 to heart and focus on things that are good, noble, reputable, admirable, pure, excellent, and praiseworthy. Praise God through your circumstance. Thank Him in advance for a fresh, new, clear mind. A mind that is available to receive every blessing He has for you.

> *Don't copy the behaviors and customs of this world, but let God transform you into a new person by changing the way you think. Then you will learn to know God's will for you, which is good and pleasing and perfect (Romans 12:2 NLT).*

10

Speak Life

"Gentle words bring life and health; a deceitful tongue crushes the spirit" (Proverbs 15:4 NLT)

I rushed home from kindergarten and told my parents what happened. They gave me a hug, and the "sticks and stones can break your bones, but words can never hurt you," spiel. "Who said that?" I asked. I remember thinking it must be a terrible person to tell a lie that big.

> *The tongue also is a fire, a world of evil among the parts of the body. It corrupts the whole body, sets the whole course of one's life on fire, and is itself set on fire by hell (James 3:6 NIV).*

Life and death are in the power of the tongue. And people can write stories on our hearts and minds that take years to erase and re-write. What I didn't realize was the power our everyday casual words have. The things we say that are automatic. The conversations we are so used to having and listening to, that we don't think about them at all. And therein lies the problem—we don't think about what we are saying, or what we take in.

God spoke the world into existence. Psalms 103:20 talks about how angels carry out God's plan by listening to His commands. One third of the angels fell from Heaven with Lucifer. This means that there are angels on both sides ready to fight for us—or against us.

The Tongue, a Creative Force, by Charles Capps, probably changed my life more than I know. It talks about the power and energy of our words, and how we have been praying and stating the wrong things. Like most things I'm sharing, before I changed my story, I would have thought it was "too much." It wasn't that it contradicted what I had been taught. I just hadn't been exposed to its spiritual truths before. To this deeper understanding of God's word.

Especially when it comes to religion, when we hear or read something that doesn't go along with what we know (or fit into our box), we are quick to judge. I've been guilty of this. As a matter of fact, if anyone were to have told me the story I told you earlier about spiritual warfare, I would have wondered about them.

Because of this, it took me a while to share my story. When I finally opened up and told a few of my Christian friends about what happened in New York with the apartment, they gave me the "let's go back to happy, I don't want to talk about this," look. I felt weird. Almost ashamed. It made me want to keep quiet. But I can't do that. Spiritual warfare is real. And when you don't know you're in a battle, you lose. When you don't understand that Satan is at work, you will misinterpret moments, situations, conversations, and circumstances—and act accordingly.

1 Peter 5:8 warns us that "our enemy the devil prowls around like a roaring lion looking for whom he can devour." It is when we are unaware of his tactics, schemes, and strategies that we are most susceptible to his ploys. The next time I shared my story, it was with some very successful leaders, trailblazers who have conquered giants and have defeated the odds. The only thing that surprised them was that the reality of spiritual warfare surprised me. Like everything else, not understanding spiritual warfare does not make it go away. Instead, it robs us of our destiny.

As I was reading *The Tongue, a Creative Force*, I reflected on my life. I heard myself being "funny."

"Watch me fall head first…"

"With my luck…"

"I'll never be able to…"

"This always happens to me!"

I heard the songs I used to sing over and over. For example, I love Karen Carpenter's voice and wanted mine to sound like hers. From the time I was five, I'd hook up my little mic, put my headphones on and sing songs like "Rainy Days and Mondays." While this song is beautiful, it's also about a girl who feels old, alone, and never fits in. It's full of longing, regrets, and "what might have been." That was half my life! When I shared this with Kimber (who we called "the lucky charm"), she said, "Hmm. I sang Zip-a-Dee-Doo-Dah."

Do I think the things I said and the songs I sang caused all my problems? Do I think they prophesied into my life? I don't think any one thing led to my anything. But when I was reading Charles Capp's book, my spirit stirred. I specifically remember a week when everything in my circumstance was in opposition to the visions God had given me. The devil of doubts was close at hand, more than ready to invade my mind. Right when I opened my mouth to start voicing my frustration, I heard *"Do not utter a single word of how you feel! Do not speak any of your doubts out loud. It will mess everything up. Do not do it. Not one word. Do not mess up your destiny."* This was God's voice. And I knew my future depended on my understanding and obeying it.

No longer do I say things like "I'm so tired, I'm sick, It's never going to..." I always speak of how I want things to be. How God told me they would be. When we do this, we are speaking life into our situation instead of reinforcing the problem. Doing this takes discipline, because it goes against everything we are used to saying, hearing, and doing. Yet what we are "used to" has gotten us, and our world, to where we are right now. Instead of bringing "Heaven to earth" by acting on what is "normal," we are contributing to the mess.

Not everyone will understand how serious this is. Not everyone wants to understand. I pray this changes. But that's all we can do.

"For nothing is hidden, except to be revealed; nor has anything been kept secret, but that it would come to light [that is, things are hidden only temporarily, until the appropriate time comes for them to be known]. If anyone has ears to hear, let him hear and heed My words." Then He said to them, "Pay attention to what you hear. By your own standard of measurement [that is, to the extent that you study spiritual truth and apply godly wisdom] it will be measured to you [and you will be given even greater ability to respond]— and more will be given to you besides"
(Mark 4: 22–24 AMP).

It is an honor for God to share His plans with you. For Him to trust you with His vision. But as much as we want them to, not everyone will "get it." Scripture warns us of this. *"Many are called, but few are chosen" (Matthew 22:14 KJV).* Your destiny doesn't depend on everyone "getting it." It depends on your response to God's word.

If God said it—you can do it. *"For verily I say unto you, that whosoever shall say unto this mountain, be thou removed, and be thou cast into the sea; and shall not doubt in his heart, but shall believe that those things which he saith shall come to pass; he shall have whatsoever he saith" (Mark 11:23 KJV).*

When we praise God in spite of our circumstance, we aren't denying the problem. We're refusing to give it control.

I have an extreme tolerance for pain. For two years, it hurt to touch my foot to the ground and all I could wear were flip flops and tennis shoes. I had worn ridiculous heels (that half the time didn't fit), for years with one of my jobs, and my foot had been stepped on countless times while clubbing and waitressing. But I was so used to ignoring the pain, biting my tongue, and smiling, that I don't know exactly how it got to this point. All I know is with each step it throbbed. So… I drank to numb the pain and kept on going. (Side note: I had some major pain pills that I rarely ever took. While beer had been okay in my house, medicine was frowned upon. I know this is not everyone's story, but I only abused what was normal to me. If you are a parent, please take this in. It is not what you say. It doesn't matter if one parent doesn't approve—whatever is accepted in your house frames the reality of what is right and wrong in your child's mind.)

Not only did it hurt to walk, it was lonely—not many people wear flip-flops and tennis shoes at night in New York City. I couldn't go to dinner with friends, I couldn't go dancing, I couldn't do much of anything. One night, I decided enough was enough. I slipped on a red silk dress. This in itself, made me feel better. Then I slipped my foot into a heel. My face turned bright red, my chest broke out in splotches, and I burst into tears. There was no way I could do this. No amount of alcohol would help. I couldn't take one step. I cried from the physical, as well as the mental, pain.

A few months after I stopped drinking, it was no longer an option—I was going to the doctor. "How have you been walking?" the doctor asked, looking at the X-rays. "There's nothing holding your toe to your foot. Your tendons and ligaments are destroyed." He recommended surgery. I saw another doctor—he recommended surgery. But even with surgery, there was only a 50% chance I'd be able to walk without pain, or wear anything other than orthopedics.

At that point, I was willing to do anything, but not being able to be on my feet for six months (which meant I wouldn't be able to work), and the whole 50% thing, I needed to think about. Meanwhile, my awesome step-dad suggested a cortisone shot. The doctor said he would do it, but cortisone shots for the rest of my life weren't an option.

The doctor gave me the shot. "Ma'am? Are you okay? Ma'am?"

I opened my eyes. "Is that all?"

"You scared me. Did that not hurt? You didn't even flinch."

"It hurt. But not half as bad as touching my foot to the ground every single day does." Five minutes later, I touched my foot to the ground and cried. I had forgotten how it felt to not be in so much pain. We do this all the time. We forget how life is supposed to feel.

I continued to get cortisone shots every six months. They worked for about four of those months. The last two were hell. One night, I was walking home from work in the rain. With each step, pain ripped through my entire being. I wanted to yell and scream. I wanted to call my mom and cry. I wanted to tell anyone who would listen how bad my foot hurt! "You shall have what you say," rang in my ears. *"For by your words you will be acquitted, and by your words you will be condemned"* (Matthew 12:37 NIV).

My tears fell like the rain, but all the way home I prophesied, "Thank You, God for healing my foot! Thank You for taking away this pain. Thank You for letting me dance in beautiful heels again! Your Word says You heal the sick, and I'm standing on Your Word with completely healed feet! You are the God of miracles, and I am Your child. Thank You, thank You, thank You for healing me. In Jesus' Name, Amen!"

I continued to watch my words and get my shots. I also had a pastor, who has the gift of healing, pray for my foot.

I was sitting in the doctor's office waiting for my shot, while the nurse asked me the normal questions. "How is the pain today?"

"Only about an eight," I replied. She gave me a look— eight is pretty high. It is. But not as high as a ten. She left the room saying the doctor would be right in.

"Sometimes healing is instant. Sometimes it takes time," echoed in my head. I believed in healing. I preached it. I was counting on it. Yet I devoted about five minutes a day praying for it. Ten minutes when the pain was worse. This didn't seem right. *My pain was only an eight.*

"The doctor's running a little behind," the nurse said, sticking her head back in. "It will be a few more minutes."

I stepped down from the bed. "That's okay."

"Do you need to reschedule?" she asked, concerned.

I moved toward the door. "No, Ma'am. God is going to heal my foot."

She gave a slight laugh. "Well…"

That was in 2014—I haven't had a shot since.

I don't know why some people are healed and others aren't. I do know there are many things that hinder our healing. Unrepented sin, unforgiveness, and unbelief are a few big ones. Yet we all know amazing, dedicated, faith-filled believers who don't experience healing. In *The Power,* author James Bramlett talks about how we live in a community of unbelief. I had never thought about that, but how true it is. Some people don't believe in anything. Others consult psychics and mediums. Then there are those who "trust" God, but rely on Google and CNN for answers. Think about how much time and energy we spend listening to doctors, scientists, psychologists, our next door neighbor—even our belief that "Jesus heals," is scattered with doubt.

In Mark 9:22–24, a desperate father takes his demon possessed son to Jesus. "If you can do anything," he asks, "please take pity on us and…"

"What do you mean, if I can?" Jesus asked. "Anything is possible if a person believes."

Immediately the boy's father exclaimed, "I do believe; help me overcome my unbelief!"

What would your life look like if everything you said came true? What would happen if you refused to doubt and only believed?

I believe in you.

11

Conquering Depression

No, despite all these things, overwhelming victory is ours through Christ, who loved us (Romans 8:37 NLT).

There are many degrees of depression. But regardless of the reasons for it, the intense feelings of nothingness can threaten to take over our lives like nothing else can. Depression steals your joy, your zest, your passion for life. It depletes your energy, hides your hope, and makes you think "this is it." Depression can make you feel like you are in hell. But notice the word that affects everything—*feel.*

Depression acts like the boss of your life. Feelings masquerade as facts. This is not a good combination, because with depression you pretty much have to do everything you don't feel like doing! When we're depressed we never want to eat right or exercise. Instead of calling friends, we isolate ourselves. And what do we do when we isolate ourselves? We think about how depressed we are. We think about every single thing that has gone wrong in our lives. We seclude ourselves and let our regrets run rampant. And the longer we regret, the more depressed we become.

Regret is anxiety, guilt, fear of the future, and shame from our past, all rolled into one. It entices us with memories of things we once loved, miss, gave away, ruined, lost, and can no longer have. It doesn't want us to think about the good things we still have, and like I shared earlier—it definitely doesn't want us to learn the lesson from the mess. Regret pulls us into a dark hole where all we see is pain. And of course, it doesn't end there. Regret leads to condemnation.

Condemnation is the opposite of conviction. (Although the enemy loves it when we confuse the two.) Conviction says, "You're missing the mark. There is a better way to live." Conviction comes through the Holy Spirit. It's the nudge, the whisper—and yes, sometimes the ache inside our hearts, that moves us to move in a different direction. It's God reaching down from Heaven saying, "I love you."

Condemnation, on the other hand, focuses on the problem. It tells us that it doesn't matter what we do because our life is already ruined. It begs us to believe that our sins are bigger than our Savior.

Have you ever noticed that the voice that tells you to do something you will later regret is the same one that condemns you when you do? The longer you listen to that voice, the longer you will stay depressed. So instead of thinking and talking about "how you feel," prophesy over yourself.

Practice Romans 4:17 and *"Calleth those things that are not, as if they were."*

Let Music Move You

Whether we want to motivate ourselves to go to the gym or are planning a romantic dinner, we put on music to "get into the mood." Yet, when we're depressed, we often choose music to match our mood! Because loneliness is such a huge part of depression, having someone—even in a song—echo how we feel validates our feelings. It gives us "the right" to feel sorry for ourselves. It also keeps us in the woe-is-me state. Our music choices, just like our words, need to reflect how we want to feel.

> Listening to songs that justify our behavior won't take us anywhere we haven't already been.

When I finally got "sick and tired of being sick and tired," I found songs that met me where I was—but spoke into where I wanted to be. I'd sleep with my headphones on, praying that the lyrics to "Let go," sung by DeWayne Woods, "I won't go back," William McDowell, and Free Chapel's "Moving Forward," would sink into my soul. What I didn't know at the time is that music really can rewire our brains! Doctors and scientists have now proven what the Bible has told us since the beginning. Music can heal, restore, revive, and bring blessings into our lives.

Resist the temptation to let your mood dictate your music. Instead, let music transform your mood, as well as your mind. Turn off the "I shouldn't have to work, revenge is what I'm after, drugs will make me feel better, sex will take the pain away" songs, and turn on the "Rocky, eye of the tiger, the fight is not over, it's time for my comeback" songs.

Walk It Out

We can't walk our problems away—but we can walk ourselves into answers. Walking brings clarity to our cluttered mind. The fresh breeze brushes hope onto our souls.

We can stop drinking. The world won't fall apart if we get fired. We can get a new job. We can live without the guy. We can lose weight. We can move again. We can survive without drugs. We aren't controlled by our past. We can change. We are strong. We are not alone.

Like the children's book, *The Little Engine That Could*, we put one foot in front of the other believing, "I *know* I can, I *know* I can…" (Yes, I changed think to know.)

A couple of years ago, I started going on prayer walks. As in, saying and/or reading my prayers out loud while I walk. At first, I did it for convenience. I'm all about multi-tasking. Now I do it because it's powerful. Regardless of how I feel when I start out, as I walk and pray out loud, my spirit stirs and pretty soon my prayers are leading me. Try it.

Manage Your Expectations

When relationships aren't working out the way we had envisioned them to, it can be depressing. However, one night while writing about how disappointed I was, the revelation hit me that this particular disappointment was my own doing. The guy I was seeing was a good person and we had fun together, but nothing in his history showed that things would be any different than they were. I had taken a little reality and mixed it with a lot of wishful thinking and was depressed that nothing was working out.

Whether it's in a relationship, a job, or your current circumstance, don't set yourself up for disappointment. There is a big difference in "hoping for the best" and living in a fantasy world.

Use Your Gifts

When I stopped pursuing a singing career, I didn't sing for years. Music had been the biggest part of my life but even my favorite songs sounded hollow. I'd try to sing in church, but no words would come. Sometimes I'd feel numb, other times it was all I could do to hold back the tears.

One night while working at a restaurant, I spontaneously chimed in on "Happy Birthday." The whole staff turned and stared at me. Later, a guest called me over to his table. "You've got some voice! What are you doing waitressing?"

"It's like a sin," said his companion.

"It is," I nodded, laughing it off.

Jesus died for our sins. Yet I was living in mine. I could have decided enough was enough, and let God "restore the years I had sown in tears." (See Psalms 126:5.) Instead, I held my tears in until I got out of there, bought a 42oz beer, and drank them away. Drowning out our sorrows and regrets with temporary fixes are just that—temporary. They relieve you only to lead you to more problems. And at that point in my life, there was no relief. The alcohol just deadened my spirit a little more.

Our gifts were given to us to glorify God. They are always incorporated into how we make a difference on this earth. Because of this, the devil does everything in his power to keep us from discovering and/or developing them. He is well versed in our insecurities, fears, and vulnerabilities, and will use them to his advantage. When we compare ourselves to others, take in negative and jealous "who do you think you are to do this" type comments, or when we justify not using our gifts at all, he sits back and smiles. For those of us determined to use our gifts, there will always be obstacles. Both internal and external. Our pride, ego, issues, ideas, even our best intentions can lead us astray. Even though I stopped acting to pursue Christian music, unconsciously, a part of me was still trying to prove something to all the people who hadn't believed in me. Making that promise to God, "I'll do whatever you say, just use me," was one of the biggest turning points in my life. (Check out "When the dream never dies," by Donna Summer.)

If you stopped using the gifts and talents God gave you, I get it. But letting pain steal your passion is a ticket to depression. Make yourself dance, sew, draw—whatever comes naturally. Take yourself on an adventure. Do something you've never done. Stir up the gifts inside you. They are one of our greatest links to our Creator. And the closer we are to our Creator, the farther away we are from depression. *"A gift opens the way for the giver and ushers him into the presence of the great"* *(Proverbs 18:16 NIV).*

Count Your Blessings

When someone nonchalantly pats you on the back and tells you to "count it all joy," it can be one of the most annoying and even hurtful things to hear. Pain is real. Loss is real. Heartache is real. If we go straight to "counting it all joy," we end up hiding from the truth—which will lead us all the way back to chapter one!

However, the Bible says, *"In everything give thanks, for this is the will of God in Christ Jesus concerning you"* *(1 Thessalonians 5:18 KJV).* God commands us to give thanks, because He wants the best for us, and counting our blessings puts us in communion with Him. *"For every good and perfect gift is from above."* (See James 1:17.) Cultivating "an attitude of gratitude" is also the one thing that psychologists, pastors, scientists, and psychiatrists agree on. It affects everything from our health to our finances.

When I was in NYC waitressing, before rushing to work, I'd write a note to myself about something I was grateful for and put it in the pocket of my apron. I would reach for a pen and feel the note. I'd get ready to take an order—there was the note. I put it in my pocket so I'd "remember," yet all day long I kept finding what I forgot was there.

Depression is like this. As much as we want to remember the good things, it distracts us. Make a list and put it where it will keep finding you.

And if you need to...

Ask For Help

If you need to see a doctor, by all means, get rid of the pride and go. If you need medicine, take it—but make sure you do need it, and don't let it become a crutch. And don't assume doctors always know what is best. There is only one doctor who always knows what is best, and His name is Jehovah Rapha—The Lord Your Healer.

"No matter what you are going through... if you have to crawl, get to church!" I heard Tim Storey say that one night at The Hollywood Bible study, and it is the one piece of advice that I've always followed. At every point in my life, I went to Bible-teaching, Spirit-filled churches. I have countless journals full of notes from some of the world's greatest pastors. Granted, I didn't act on all of the notes I took—but seeds were being planted. God's word, His knowledge, and His wisdom were all inside me. I just had to make the choice to put it all into action. Thank God, I finally did.

When I moved back to LA, I ran into a friend whom I hadn't seen in ten years, who told me about a church on Melrose and Labrea. It was close to where I was staying, so I went. As soon as I walked through the door, I knew it was where I was supposed to be. It was as if the pastor was preaching from one of my old journals. (Not the parts I wrote, the parts God wrote through me.)

Each Sunday, I watch swarms of people go to the altar for prayer and I wonder what it would have been like to have had help, to have had prayer warriors praying for me. I wonder what it would have been like not to go through my journey alone.

Of course, I asked for prayer many times during my journey. But I was never honest about how rough the journey had become. No one knew. Did it work out? Yes, because God works all things out for good for those who are called according to His purpose (read Romans 8:28). But with everything I know now about the power in prayer, I would have had my breakthrough much sooner. Maybe I'm wrong. Maybe I'm not. Either way, all I can do is praise God and share everything with you that He shared with me.

⁓ ⁓ ⁓ ⁓ ⁓ ⁓

I've been depressed to the point where getting up to get a sip of water was an effort. I fought hard. I'd sleep with my headphones on, blaring praise music in my ears. I made myself go to the gym, to church, to work, I went to counseling… I did a lot of right things. But I also tried to fill the hole in my heart with earthly things. Namely alcohol. I'm not going to say it never helped, because it did. There were moments when it eased my pain. It helped me "not to think." It also prolonged my healing. (And could have killed me.)

You have to fight depression head on. This means dealing with your backstory, understanding, and changing the way you think, renewing your mind (every thought that is not a "good, noble, moving you forward" thought has to go), replacing your truth with God's truth, letting go of the past (which is *not* the same thing as dealing with your backstory), and doing what is right, regardless of how you feel.

There are moments when depression tries to sneak back into my life. Some days it chases me. But it is the exception, not the norm. However, a couple of summers ago, a "thunderstorm" came swooping down on me. One that begged to undo me. Unlike many before, this one was none of my doing. I was living by faith, pursuing purpose, and in constant communication with God. Yet the depression that came upon me was as heavy as it was when I was a disaster. I lay in bed not breathing. I picked up my Bible. The scriptures I had underlined and highlighted, the very ones that spoke life into my life, stared back at me. A heaviness like a pound of bricks lay on my chest. I told myself everything I'm telling you, everything I know to be true, but it didn't matter. A horrible, crushing emptiness was suffocating me. The feeling was all too familiar, and I was scared. "God what is going on?"

This is what I heard. *"It is a spirit, and you have to kick it out. It is from the enemy. You have the authority to demand it to leave."*

I pictured myself fighting for my life that day on 29th Street and Madison Avenue. And right then I spoke to depression, just like I had the devil. "Get out of me! Get out of my heart! Get out of my mind! Get your hands off my emotions! Get off my property! Get off the destiny God has for me! Get off my family! Get out of my relationships! I am a child of God, created in Christ Jesus. I have the Holy Spirit living inside me, and by the blood of Jesus I am free. So go back to hell where you belong!"

Depression is a spirit. It has a voice. And it had tried to steal mine for way too long.

> *My people are destroyed from lack of knowledge.*
> *Because you have rejected knowledge, I also reject*
> *you as my priests; because you have ignored the*
> *law of your God, I also will ignore your children*
> *(Hosea 4:6 NLT).*

As a child, being scared is fun. We love the rush of adrenaline that beats through our body. We make believe we're ghosts and goblins, acting out the scary scenes we read and see on TV. Being scared is safe, for we know it's just pretend and that our parents are there to protect us.

There have been countless times when I walked into a room, met someone at work, and entered into conversations, when my body tensed, saying, *"Something's wrong."* Because everything looked fine and no one else seemed to be feeling what I was feeling, I ignored my instincts. Every time—even when I wish they hadn't been, my instincts were right. Staying in these situations was costly. Some of them could have been deadly. But see, I had talked myself out of being scared so often as a child, that it was normal to ignore my rapid heartbeat, the weird lump in my throat, the tightening of my chest, my churning stomach, and all of the other signals our body gives us to alert us that something is wrong.

Spiritual warfare was never talked about in my house—and it definitely wasn't mentioned in church. The devil loves this. He depends on our staying ignorant. On cold, rainy days my friends and I would turn the basement into a haunted house. When we got older we'd have séances at slumber parties. Of course, we had no idea what we were doing—which is exactly what the devil and all his entities count on.

We have got to stop closing our eyes to the parts of the Bible that we don't understand or that interfere with "what has always been okay." We tell children that witches and apparitions (known as ghosts), aren't real. Yet from Genesis through Revelation the Bible talks about how very real they are. They are God's enemies. Which makes them our enemies.

> *"Who will rise up for me against the wicked?*
> *Who will take a stand for me against evildoers?"*
> *(Psalm 94:16 NIV)*

Each year, on Oct. 31, thousands of good parents let their children go trick-or-treating saying, "They're just having fun." Looking back, I wonder how much of my depression, the fear, the all-consuming thoughts—the battle for my life—stemmed from "just having fun." As individuals, as Christians, as a church, and as a nation, it is time to grow up. This is not a game, and everything we do stirs up something.

> *"Finally, be strong in the Lord and in His mighty*
> *power. Put on the full armor of God, so that you*
> *can take your stand against the devil's schemes"*
> *(Ephesians 6:10–11 NIV).*

When people used to say, "Put on your armor," I had no idea what they were talking about. Now I don't get out of bed without it!

> *Dear Father, thank You for the Helmet of*
> *Salvation that protects me from lies, half-truths,*
> *and doubts the enemy throws my way. Thank You*
> *for the Breastplate of Righteousness that guards*
> *my heart—I'm not controlled by, nor am I scared*
> *of emotions. Thank You for the Sword of the*
> *Spirit—Your mighty Word. Thank You for the*
> *Shield of Faith that protects my heart, my dreams,*
> *my vision, and allows me to see past my circum-*
> *stances. Thank You for the Belt of Truth remind-*
> *ing me to do what is right consistently, not just*
> *when it's convenient. And God, thank You for my*
> *completely healed feet that walk by Faith and not*
> *by sight!*

The official prayer is found in Ephesians 6:13–18. Make it your own, and put your armor on daily. Stand firm against the schemes of the enemy. Ask God to fight for you—and use the weapons He's already given you. Depression has no right on, or in, your life. Your mind, heart, body, and soul, your home, your property, and your relationships, are protected by the blood of Jesus. Tell the enemy that. Make him flee. In Jesus' Name.

> *I remind you that it is written,*
> *"Greater is He that is in you,*
> *than he that is in the world."*
> *(Read 1 John 4:4.)*

12

Just Believe

"For I know the plans I have for you," declares the Lord.
"Plans to prosper you and not to harm you, plans to
give you a hope and a future" (Jeremiah 29:11 NIV).

When God gives us an assignment, a God-sized dream, it's always bigger than us and never just about us. It will take more than we have. It might not make sense, and it won't come with a ten year plan.

In Luke 1 verses 37–39, God sends an angel to tell Mary that she is highly favored and going to have a baby. The angel continues, saying His name will be Jesus and that He will be the Savior of the world. Mary's response: "I am the Lord's servant. May it be as you have said."

Can you imagine if God had told her that the Son He was giving her would be persecuted most of His life? That He would be hated, spat at, lied about—that even His best friends would betray Him? Mary wasn't told the price her Son would pay for being the Savior of our lives. That He would be left to die hanging on a cross. If God had told her everything… I wonder if she would have said yes.

> God knows His plans for us.
> He also knows they will overwhelm us.
> He knows how much we can take—
> And when we can take it.
> He plants a seed in us.
> He gives us a vision. He asks for our trust.
> He asks for our "yes."

Many times we block our blessings. We don't take the first step toward God's plan for our lives, because we base His plan on our reality. We rationalize things to death. We listen to the wrong voice. We think our way out of our destiny. When I realized I was writing a book and got excited, the enemy instantly spewed out reasons why it wouldn't and couldn't work. All of them made sense! Based on what I had been through, based on my past, even where I was at that very minute, most of the world would have unknowingly agreed with the devil—I was wasting my time.

> *Jesus looked at them and said, "With people this is impossible, but with God all things are possible" (Matthew 19:26 NIV).*

There is provision, miracles, wisdom, and favor packaged into God's plan for our life. But we have to step out in faith in order to experience it. We have to do the work and trust Him for the results. For there is always a bigger picture.

As soon as I completed *Believe,* I sent it to publishers. I couldn't wait for every middle grader in the universe to get their hands on this amazing book! Not only was it not ready, I was not ready. God wanted my obedience. He needed to know that when I wrote the entire book in the wrong format, that when my computer broke down, that when I lost my job, my savings, and was being attacked from every side, that I wasn't going to give up or go back to old habits. How was I going to walk out every rejection? Could I hear His voice between the chaos and the confusion? Did I know the difference between "giving up" and putting something down for a season because God said to?

God needed to make sure that this time, I was in love with the Dream Giver, not the dream. God was making sure I was trustworthy, and in the process, not only was I learning to rely on Him completely, I was also learning to trust myself again.

Looking back at Mary's life, what part of her story is the hardest for you to believe? Is it that she was pregnant without ever having sex? That an angel spoke to her? Maybe it's that she was just a simple girl. For me, and maybe you can identify, it's that she just said, "Yes!" Not, "Well, let me think about it," or "How in the world is this going to happen? Is Joseph still going to marry me? What will people think? I mean, it sounds cool but I need more details." Mary didn't ask any of the "normal" questions. She just said *yes,* and let God take care of the rest.

It's incomprehensible to our human minds what God can do, and how He fits the pieces of our lives together. Sometimes it's the most difficult chapters (the ones that in the moment, feel like they're meant for someone else's life) that end up getting us back on track and propelling us into our destiny.

One day, you will look back on your life and see how God took your mess and weaved it into His master plan. The recall will be amazing.

13

It's a Journey

Your life is a journey you must travel with a deep consciousness of God (1 Peter 1:18 MSG).

Initially, our bodies and minds don't know what to do with change. Digging deep, dealing with our backstory, and letting go of life-long habits makes us extra sensitive. Make sure you are hearing what is being said in the moment, versus what you've heard in the past. Take an extra second before you respond. Ask yourself things like, "Am I really upset about the situation at hand, or is the situation triggering a learned response from a hidden memory?"

Change takes time. It takes work. But it is work you are worth.

Hold On to God's Promises.
Let Go of What's Holding You Back.
Move Forward Despite What's in the Way.

We can't hold on to everything. Yet we must hold on to something. Hold on to the good part of life. Remember what your family and friends did (and do) that is right. Hold on to the lessons you learned while going through the fire: *Look for the lesson.*

When opposition struck in the past, I'd pray, "God, please just let this be over." I still ask for it to be over! But not until I recognize the problem behind the problem. Not until I see the truth. Not until I come to a higher level of understanding, a stronger sense of self. Not until the bar has been raised on my life. Not until I have a closer relationship with our Creator, and a deeper understanding of who I am in Him. Not until this part of my journey makes sense and propels me into the next, and better, chapter.

There is a promise inside your pain. A purpose amidst the problem. This does not mean that what you're going through is God's will. It means He can make beauty out of ashes and turn mourning into dancing. God will work all things out for our good. (Read Isaiah 61:3 and Romans 8:28.) But we have to cooperate with our comeback. We have to co-labor with God. He will readily hold our hand, but we have to take the steps.

Let Go of "This is how it's always been."

Let go of the grudge. Your pride. Your regrets. Whatever is in the way of your being the best version of yourself, let it go.

Life is short, and there are so many battles we must, and are supposed to, fight. However, we spend a lot of time avoiding the ones that matter and trying to win the ones that don't. Our ego gets in the way. We find reasons to avoid spending time with the people who matter most to us and instead hang around people who agree with us. We pattern our lives so that we feel good, hiding from our own truth. Our lifestyle becomes so "normal" that rarely will anyone question it. Let "normal" go. Whether you see it right now or not, it is hurting you. It is holding you back. You were made to be extraordinary.

> The righteous keep moving forward
> and those with clean hands become
> stronger and stronger (Job 17:9 NLT).

It's true that until you look in the mirror and get honest with yourself about what needs changing, nothing will change. But once you've done that, focus on what you are doing right and then make the next right move. But when you do—don't expect applause.

There is nothing quite like the feeling of doing the work that change requires, only to have people see you as being the same. Some people don't want to accept you've changed because it makes them feel guilty they haven't. Some are over-joyed you've changed—yet they can't accept it. For reasons of their own, it's easier to see you in the light of your past. Some people need time, and then there are those whom you will never be able to please.

I know firsthand how much this hurts. I also know that the stronger the relationship was (or is supposed to be), the more apt you are to give up. To go back. Don't do this. Please don't do this. God put you on this earth with a purpose that is independent of whether anyone understands how much you've grown, how far you've come, and how strong and beautiful you truly are. God sees you. He's holding your hand and cheering you on. He has big plans for you.

When Your Vision Gets Blurry— Sometimes All You Have Is What God Said.

When everything in your circumstance says, "it's not happening," when the "I can't take anymore" feeling is taking over, close your eyes and picture the moment when you knew you could change. Remember the vision God gave you. The miracles you've experienced. Think about the *strangers* that appeared at just the right time and said exactly what you needed to hear. Remember how far you've come—and what it took to get you here.

When I first stopped drinking, the thought "you so deserve a drink," would frequently enter my mind. Instead of agreeing, I shut the thought down with, "No, I deserve a healthy life that I'm proud of." Instead of thinking about what you are giving up, think about what you are gaining.

When your vision gets blurry, put on your Faith glasses. *"Now faith is being sure of what we hope for and certain of what we do not see" (Hebrews 11:1 NIV).*

Don't Break Down—Break Through

In the beginning, we know exactly what we need to breakaway from. We have a goal. Many people think when they reach their goal, that's it. You are not most people. You're just not. Breakthroughs lead us to our new beginnings. They take us to new levels. And for each new level, there is a new ceiling. We have to keep climbing. Seeking. Reaching. Learning. Growing. And the higher we climb, the greater the tests. *And the rewards.*

I've experienced more tests (a very nice word for attacks) while writing this book, than I have in years. The harder the enemy hits, the more I understand how important it is that I write *Change Your Story.*

From the minute you decide to change, the enemy will be after you. He knows the strength you will find when you decide to be the highest version of yourself. He knows what God has in store for you. This is not something you need to be scared of, or focus on. You just need to be aware, arm yourself accordingly, and know that with Christ you are unstoppable!

Get used to being uncomfortable. Get used to opposition. Get used to being the world shaker and history maker God created you to be. Take hold of 1 John 4:4, *"Greater is He that is inside of me, than he that is in the world."* Know that God will never leave you or forsake you. In your darkest hours He is here for you. (See Hebrews 13:5.)

God is looking for people who won't give up. Those who have been through hell and keep getting up. People who hold on to hope. Think about your favorite movie. The villain has internalized his pain. He causes destruction due to his unresolved conflicts and faulty thinking. The hero (in this case you), decides that he is stronger than the battle. Not only are you breaking out of this mess, but you will also be an inspiration to everyone still in one.

"Everyone" Includes The Person You Still Can't Forgive.

We say the words "I forgive you," and think it's a done deal. But as we progress, our need to forgive on a deeper level increases.

I don't know about you, but I can forgive those "who know not what they do," a whole lot easier than those who absolutely do (or at least should) know what they are doing! And I get "loving the unlovable," but how do we love the very lovable, yet messed up person who refuses to change and hurts everyone in his or her path?

"Therefore, I tell you, her many sins have been forgiven— as her great love has shown. But whoever has been forgiven little loves little" (Luke 7:47 NIV). When you've moved through pain, when you've experienced God's love, mercy, and forgiveness, you understand how much the other person needs it. You can separate yourself from the hurt. You can ask for forgiveness, even when it's not your fault. No matter how wrong things were (or are), you don't want to bring any more wrong into the

picture. You know what guilt does to the soul, and that love is the only thing that heals.

But remember, we love to love. We forgive, because we have been forgiven. We eat right to be healthy. We stop taking drugs, drinking, denying, cutting, cheating, overspending, and giving our heart to the wrong people, because God has a purpose and plan for our lives that depends on it.

You can choose to change. You can love the unlovable and forgive the unforgivable, but it doesn't mean everyone else will. No matter how much you've changed, or how many times others promise to change, you can't change anyone else. You can't make them forgive you. You can't make them love you. You can't make them see the truth. Not understanding this—or at least accepting this, can lead us down a very lonely road.

Renew your mind and put your heart, time, and energy into making the changes you need to make, in order to fulfill your calling on earth.

> Let us not become weary in doing good,
> for at the proper time we will reap a harvest
> if we don't give up (Galatians 6:9 NIV).

You will probably get frustrated, tired, and overwhelmed. You might cry a lot. And as soon as you think you are better, don't be surprised if a sense of guilt and emptiness… a longing I can't even put into words, hits you. This is especially likely if you are breaking free from an addiction.

No matter how many right things you do, you won't always be treated accordingly. You will see others doing the wrong things (worse things than you ever did) and succeeding. "Why bother?" will enter your mind more than once. "Bother" because you are worth it.

> *"You are God's handiwork, created in Christ Jesus to do good works, which God prepared in advance for you to do." (Read Ephesians 2:10.)*

14

Becoming Your Own Hero

Heroes hold on to God Dreams. They visualize the life they want and make changes accordingly. They find ways to reinvent themselves, and trust that the best is yet to come.

Mother Teresa started her ministry on the streets with no home and no money. Martin Luther King Jr. lived in a society that persecuted him. Have you heard of David Wilkerson or Nick Vujicic? Wilkerson pastored a small church in Pennsylvania. It was growing and doing well, but he felt God wanted him to go into NYC and help the prostitutes and drug addicts. Nick Vujicic was born without any limbs. In his book, *Life without Limbs,* he talks about contemplating suicide as a child. Instead, he turned his disability into his ability.

Based on their circumstance, our heroes could have easily thought, "How could I ever...? Who am I to think I could...?" Thank God, they saw a bigger picture.

Mother Teresa ministered to the lepers. She went into the slums of Calcutta and fed the homeless and the poorest of the poor. Martin Luther King Jr. was the most important voice of the American civil rights movement. David Wilkerson's obedience to God's voice birthed a church in Times Square, where over 8,000 people representing more than one hundred nationalities gather weekly. He also founded Teen Challenge, a recovery program for anyone with life-controlling addictions. It has one of the highest success rates of any secular or Christian program in the United States and is one of the best in the world. Nick Vujicic has shared his message of hope with over six-million people in fifty-seven countries.

I guarantee you that they, as well as every other person we admire and aspire to be like, had moments of, "I can't take anymore. I'm tired of fighting and not seeing results. The uncertainty, the criticism, the rejections—I'm worn out!" They had their moments. But they didn't let the moments define them or determine their actions. When faced with difficulty they knew they had a choice and they kept moving forward. Our heroes' purposes were greater than their pain. Stronger than their insecurities. Bolder than their fears. They knew that life wasn't about them.

We all know people who defy the odds.
We also know those who wear statistics
like a scarlet letter.

Our daily decisions—the seemingly insignificant ones—as well as the things we ignore, either guide us into greatness, or lead us down the wrong path. The amazing thing is, at any point, we can make a U-turn. We can turn around, start anew, and choose a different path. It's all about choices. It really is.

In chapter five, we talked about the "All is lost" moment. The cliffhanger moment when the fate of our favorite character hangs in the air. The trials, tribulations, and triumphs he or she has faced brought them to this moment. But it is what they choose to do from this point forward that determines the outcome of the story.

> *"I press on to reach the end of the race and receive the heavenly prize for which God, through Christ Jesus is calling us" (Philippians 3:14 NLT).*

The heroes I mentioned share many similarities. They're tenacious, brave, courageous, loyal, confident, and daring. They also knew ("know" in Nick's case) that without God's guidance, wisdom, forgiveness, grace, and supernatural protection, they would never accomplish great and mighty things. They were wise enough to know that in their "All is lost" moment, alone, they might have chosen differently.

"Becoming Your Own Hero" isn't about being heroic. It's about co-laboring with God to fulfill the purpose He created you for. It's letting the greatness inside you (the Holy Spirit) take over. It's letting your light shine through the darkness. It's releasing the love and beauty that is within you. It's about using your gifts and talents to glorify God—making His name known.

Not everyone will believe you can change your story. Not everyone can comprehend that you will be the person in your family who graduates college, who gets a Masters, who breaks the chain of addiction. They may not believe that people will come to Christ because of you. That your story will bring God glory. They may not believe that you have the potential to change the world and make history.

Not everyone has vision. Not everyone will let Faith write their story. But you are not everyone—you are the only person who can play the part God designed you for. If you don't know what that part is right now, don't worry. When you take action on everything you've been reading, your destiny will reveal itself.

No matter how it reads right now, your story is a masterpiece waiting to be discovered.

CHANGE YOUR STORY CHECKLIST

1. Claim Your Identity

* I have the mind of Christ (1 Corinthians 2:16).
* I am a friend of Jesus (John 15:15).
* I am a new creature in Christ (2 Corinthians 5:17).
* I am more than a conqueror through Him who strengthens me (Romans 8:37).
* I am raised up with Christ and seated in Heavenly places (Ephesians 2:6; Colossians 2:12).
* I am extraordinary and greatly loved by God (Ephesians 2:4).
* I am a partaker of His divine nature (2 Peter 1:3–4).
* I am far from oppression, and fear does not come near me (Isaiah 54:14).
* I am a joint-heir with Christ (Romans 8:17).
* I can do everything through Christ who gives me strength (Philippians 4:13).
* I am an overcomer by the blood of the Lamb and the word of my testimony (Revelation 12:11).
* I am the temple of the Holy Spirit; I am not my own (1 Corinthians 6:19).
* I am the head and not the tail; above and not beneath (Deuteronomy 28:13).
* God meets all my needs according to the riches of His glory in Jesus Christ (Philippians 4:19).
* I am the righteousness of God in Jesus Christ (2 Corinthians 5:21).

2. Know Your Objective

What do you want more than anything in life? The answer to this is your "overall objective" and every other competing emotion, feeling, and desire has to bow down and get out of the way of it.

You also have immediate short term objectives. While they may not seem to matter in regards to your overall objective— they do. *Everything* needs to be in alignment with your overall objective.

3. Be Intentional

Know your "why." Are the actions you are getting ready to take, the decisions you're about to make, the words you *want* to say, going to bring you closer or take you farther away from your overall objective? In other words, what is the purpose behind each action, decision, and conversation? What is your "why?"

4. Take A Step Back

When situations, relationships, and decisions are "in our face," whether good or bad, our emotions are heightened. The intensity of the moment makes it almost impossible to see anything other than the moment we are in. If we're not careful, we forget everything we know.

Don't do this—you've worked too hard. Take a step back. Take a breath. Take a walk. Pause and Pray. Ask God for clarity *before* you move forward. The decisions you make in these moments will forever affect your life.

5. Be An Asset

Instead of always being the person who needs something, be the one who offers something. Have a "What can I do for you?" attitude. And mean it.

6. Be Open

"For I am about to do something new. See, I have already begun. Do you not see it? I will make a pathway through the wilderness. I will create rivers in the dry wasteland"
(Isaiah 43:16–19 NLT).

When God gave me the first dream I shared, I knew it was important and was trying to wake myself up so I could write it down. But He specifically told me "not to move," that I would remember it. A year later, when He gave me what is now *Believe,* He was adamant that I wake up and write it down.

Sometimes we are so focused on what God said the last time, we miss what He's saying this time. God moves in mysterious ways. And He is always moving.

7. Expect Great Things

In *Believe,* the main character is a vivacious twelve-year-old. After having her hopes and dreams crushed, she stumbles upon an amazing opportunity. But instead of being excited, she's shocked and full of unbelief, thinking, "It's crazy. There's no time, I've never done this before." Her new, older friend tells her sometimes we live so strongly in our disappointments, we don't see the amazing possibilities right in front of us. That sometimes they're the greatest opportunities thus far, but we're so busy looking behind, that we miss out. Of course, our twelve year old hero instantly decides there's NO WAY that's happening to her.

A lot has happened since we were twelve. Rejections, misplaced trust, financial concerns, addictions, broken hearts… all of these things make it hard to believe that something spectacular is coming our way. Yet Psalms 126:5–6 and Job 8:7 assure us that God will restore the years we've sown in tears, and that our latter days can be greater than our former ones.

God is already doing a "new thing," but we have to have faith to perceive, and eyes that believe.

8. Know Thyself

Don't set yourself up for failure. Know your trigger points. Don't put yourself in compromising circumstances by walking into the lion's den. Treat yourself like the best friend you ever (or never) had.

9. No Excuses

The blame game gets us nowhere. We are responsible for the choices we make. If you make a wrong move, own it. None of us are perfect and change takes time. Look at the situation long enough to know where you went wrong. Ask God for forgiveness and then "go and sin no more."

If we confess our sins, He is faithful and just and will forgive us our sins and purify us from all unrighteousness (1 John 1:9 NIV).

10. Master Your Time

You don't have time to be mad. You don't have time for negative thoughts. You don't have time to dwell on the past. And you definitely don't have time for "busy." If what you are doing doing isn't in line with your overall objective, stop doing it. Stop talking about it. Stop thinking about it.

11. Stop Comparing

There will always be someone who has it worse than you, and there will always be someone who has it better. This is irrelevant. Your story is your story—and it's waiting on you.

12. Pray

Prayer is the most powerful, yet overlooked, weapon we have. Praying makes us wise, courageous, tenacious, and unstoppable. It gives us confidence and energy, sharpens our discernment, protects us from discouragement, provides direction, helps us distinguish between busyness and fruitfulness, brings calm to our storms, and opens doors of opportunity like nothing else can.

It is through prayer that we find the strength to stand against depression, rejection, temptation, fear, and every other negative behavior and emotion. Praying helps us discover our purpose; it heals our hearts, renews our spirits… And yet, it is so much more. Prayer brings us into the greatest relationship we will ever have. It connects us to our Maker—our Father, our Healer, our Redeemer, our Master, our Savior… A Friend like no other.

If you have never invited Jesus into your heart, or if you would like to re-dedicate your life to Him, I urge you to make the following prayer your own.

Dear Father, I come to You in the name of Jesus. I am so sorry for my sins and the life I have lived. I need Your forgiveness. I believe that Your only begotten Son, Jesus Christ, came to save my life. That He shed His blood on the cross at Calvary and died for my sins.

Romans 10:9 says that if I confess, "Jesus is Lord," and believe in my heart that God raised Jesus from the dead, that I will be saved. Right now, I am accepting and declaring that Jesus is the Lord of my life. With all my heart, I believe God raised Jesus from the dead, and accept Him as my personal Savior. According to His Word, right now, I am saved.

Thank You Jesus for Your grace that has saved me from my sins, and Your Holy blood that washes me white as snow. I understand that Your grace is not a license to sin, but rather it leads me to repentance. Thank You for saving me from so many things. Some of which I will never know. Thank You for saving me from myself, and giving me another chance to truly live. With Your grace, and by Your Word, I will do the work that renewing my mind will take. Thank You in advance for my transformed life! Thank You for Your Spirit that lives inside me. May Your every Word be a "light unto my path," leading me only where You would have me go, so that I may bring glory and honor to You alone.

Thank You for living for me, dying for me, and giving me eternal life. In Jesus' Name I pray, Amen.

You are now officially hooked up with The Greatest Counselor of all time. And with Him you have the strength to make every change you will ever need to make.

> *"For the creation waits in eager expectation for the children of God to be revealed"*
> *(Romans 8:19 NIV).*

Scriptures to Stand On

And the peace of God, which transcends all understanding, will guard your hearts and your minds in Christ Jesus (Philippians 4:7 NIV).

I keep asking that the God of our Lord Jesus Christ, the glorious Father, may give you the Spirit of wisdom and revelation, so that you may know Him better. I pray that the eyes of your heart may be enlightened in order that you may know the hope to which He has called you, the riches of His glorious inheritance in His holy people (Ephesians 1:17-18 NIV).

And the peace of God, which transcends all understanding, will guard your hearts and your minds in Christ Jesus (Philippians 4:7 NIV).

Don't lie to each other, for you have stripped off your old sinful nature and all its wicked deeds. Put on your new nature, and be renewed as you learn to know your Creator and become like him (Colossians 3:9-10 NLT).

But we have power over all these things through Jesus who loves us so much (Romans 8:37 NLV).

Come to me, all you who are weary and burdened, and I will give you rest. Take My yoke upon you and learn from Me, for I am gentle and humble in heart, and you will find rest for your souls (Matthew 11:28-29 NIV).

"For our struggle is not against flesh and blood, but against the rulers, against the authorities, against the powers of this dark world and against the spiritual forces of evil in the heavenly realms" (Ephesians 6:12 NIV).

When there is no revelation, people cast off restraint; but blessed is the one who heeds wisdom's instruction
(Proverbs 29:18 NIV).

"For I know the plans I have for you," declares the Lord, "plans to prosper and not to harm you, plans to give you a hope and a future" (Jeremiah 29:11 NIV).

"In your anger do not sin, do not let the sun go down on you while you are still angry, and do not give the devil a foothold" (Ephesians 4:26-27 NIV).

Guard your heart above all else, for it determines the course of your life (Proverbs 4:23 NLT).

Create in me a clean heart, Oh God, and renew a right spirit within me (Psalm 55:10 ESV).

Remember what it says: "Today when you hear His voice, do not let your hearts be hardened as Israel did when they rebelled" (Hebrews 3:15 NLT).

I will give thanks to the LORD, with my whole heart; I will recount all of your wonderful deeds (Psalm 9:1 ESV).

The LORD is close to the brokenhearted; He rescues those whose spirits are crushed (Psalms 34:18 NLT).

God blesses those whose hearts are pure, for they will see God (Matthew 5:8 NLT).

Trust in the Lord with all your heart and lean not on your own understanding; in all your ways submit to Him, and He will make your paths straight (Proverbs 3:5-6 NIV).

Do not be afraid—I am with you! I am your God—let nothing terrify you! I will make you strong and help you; I will protect you and save you (Isaiah 41:10 GNT).

Submit yourselves, then, to God. Resist the devil and he will flee from you (James 4:7 NIV).

"Peace I leave with you; my peace I give you. I do not give to you as the world gives. Do not let your hearts be troubled and do not be afraid" (John 14:27 NIV).

Walk with the wise and become wise; associate with fools and get in trouble (Proverbs 13:20 NLT).

Each time He said, "My grace is all you need. My power works best in weakness." So now I am glad to boast about my weaknesses, so that the power of Christ can work through me (2 Corinthians 12:9 NLT).

Let us not become weary in doing good, for at the proper time we will reap a harvest if we do not give up (Galatians 6:9 NIV).

The perfect time to change your story will never come.
It is right here. Right now.
Put on your armor. Stay strong.
And let the praises begin!

*One of the biggest
reasons I never asked
for help, is because I
didn't want to be a
burden on anyone.
When someone asks
for prayer or opens up
and confides in me…
Burdened? I'm honored.
It's part of the blessing
and responsibility
of being free.
Thank you for reading
this book. Now go out
and change your story.*

Kirstin Leigh

To find out about Kirstin's latest projects or to have her speak at your next event, visit Kirstinleigh.biz

You can also follow Kirstin on:
facecbook.com/KirstinLeighWriter
twitter.com/KirstinLeigh3
instagram.com/KirstinLeigh3

Made in the USA
Monee, IL
11 July 2022